ONE-OFF

INDEPENDENT RETAIL DESIGN

CLARE DOWDY

LAURENCE KING

Published in 2008
by Laurence King Publishing Ltd
361-373 City Road
London EC1V 1LR
Tel +44 (0)20 7841 6900
Fax +44 (0)20 7841 6910
e-mail enquiries@laurenceking.co.uk
www.laurenceking.co.uk

Text © Clare Dowdy 2008
This book was produced by Laurence King Publishing Ltd

A catalogue record for this book is available from the British Library.

ISBN-13: 978-1-85669-519-0

Designed by James Branch

Printed in China

ONE-OFF

INDEPENDENT RETAIL DESIGN

CLARE DOWDY

LAURENCE KING PUBLISHING

CONTENTS

FASHION AND ACCESSORIES

Random Gems

PRETENDERS AND GUERRILLA STORES

ONE-OFF
INTRODUCTION

'Retailers I find interesting are small, local and niche,' claims Tom Dixon, the creative director of Habitat, one of the most well-known chains in the UK, adding that 'where everything else is corporate, the single voice is appealing and attractive'.

This view is surely shared by shoppers around the world and yet, increasingly, the small, local and niche is being replaced by the uniform, homogenous and mass market. Success in retail is now measured in the number of outlets of any one brand, and everyone, it seems, is going for growth as they chase ever better economies of scale. The obvious examples are in the supermarket sector, with Tesco, Wal-Mart, Carrefour and their ilk pursuing global dominance. As these continue to spread their nets, and offer a wider range of products to boot, it's not just the local food shops which are under threat. Everything from fashion boutiques to electrical retailers is being squeezed out.

Eric Schlosser charted the decline of the independent store in his book Fast Food Nation,
where he saw the fast-food model being adopted by retail in general. 'The basic thinking behind fast food has become the operating system of today's retail economy, wiping out small businesses, obliterating regional differences, and spreading identical stores throughout the country like a self-replicating code. America's main streets and malls now boast the same Pizza Huts and Taco Bells, Gaps and Banana Republics, Starbucks and Jiffy Lubes, Foot Lockers, Snip N' Chips, Sunglass Huts, and HobbyTown USAs. Almost every facet of American life has now been franchised or chained. A person can now go from the cradle to the grave without spending a nickel at an independently owned business.'

This phenomenon is described as 'the chaining of America' in Oliver James's book Affluenza. 'By using economics of scale in purchasing and distribution, and being able to stay in the market even at a loss, these monolithic retailers can drive out competition within a year, and in some cases sooner.' But this is not just a US problem. This process has also been charted in the UK by

Right
Labour and Wait, a quirky one-off store in London's East End, acts as an anti-dote to the homogenous retailing of many of today's chains.

Joanna Blythman. In <u>Shopped – The Shocking Power of British Supermarkets</u>, she describes how most UK towns have become 'trolley towns, shaped by the grocery chains that dominate them', which leaves just 'charity shops, video shops and, in more affluent centres, branches of large retail chains'.

According to the report <u>High Street Britain: 2015</u>, half of the 278,630 high street shops in the UK were owned and managed by a sole trader in 2004; and 103,000 had fewer than five employees. Yet the All-Party Parliamentary Group for Small Shops expressed concerns that these retailers may cease trading as soon as 2015. While the damage has already been done to many of the shopping streets in the affluent West, for the developing world it's only a matter of time.

As Euromonitor said in its report <u>Retailing in India: A Nation of Shopkeepers</u>, 'India has sometimes been called a nation of shopkeepers. This epithet has its roots in the huge number of retail enterprises in India, which totalled over 12 million in 2003. About 78 per cent of these are small family businesses utilizing only household labour. Inevitably, modernization of the Indian retail sector will be reflected in rapid growth in sales of supermarkets, department stores and hypermarkets. This is because of the growing preference of the affluent and upper middle classes for shopping at these types of retail stores, given the conveniences they offer such as shopping ambience, variety and a single-point source for purchases. Hence, sales from these large format stores are predicted to expand at growth rates ranging from 24 per cent to 49 per cent per year during 2003 to 2008.'

Similarly, in Russia, Euromonitor predicts 'the further reduction of unorganized retailing and the construction of new retail areas, including large-format commercial and entertainment complexes'. Meanwhile, in Thailand, 'the inevitable trend is that traditional retailers such as small "mom and pop" stores and wet markets are gradually making their irreversible exit from the Thai retail trade, replaced by a plethora of new modern retailers.' And so it goes on, from Seoul to Sofia.

Below left and right
The fast-food model of architectural uniform-ity, as seen in Taco Bell on the right, has been mimicked by such retail chains as WalMart, below.

Countries that are perceived as having plenty of retail growth attract developers with their sights set on shopping malls. By their very nature, these tend to cater for the chains, as few independent shops can afford the rent. It sounds bleak, but against all the odds, there is a new generation of one-offs that is bucking these trends. In his book A Good Life, Leo Hickman claims that in the UK, 'A new movement is afoot to bring back more local shops and support existing ones in towns, high streets and village centres.'

But it's not just in the over-chained West that this new-style, one-off retail, is gathering pace. From Bangalore to Berlin, entrepreneurs are opening their own shops. Often as not, they have a yearning to run their own business and a passion for their stock. Some have former retail experience; others are alarmingly naïve about the sector. Among the thousands every year who set up shop, many will position themselves in such a way as to differentiate themselves from the chains that surround them. 'The secret of success for the small retailer… is to offer consumers something

different, something better and something targeted very precisely at a particular portion of the market,' explains Kevin Hawkins, the British Retail Consortium's director general. Richard Perks, director of retail research at Mintel, backs this up: 'You can start as a niche player of some sort and hope to spot a gap in the market.' For Chip Howes, founder of the Powerline 6 fashion store in California, 'all the mass efficiency in retail (Wal-Mart, Target) is fascinating in its complexity, but lacks individuality. This opens a big, fat door for new expression in boutique retail spaces. The centre is dead.'

The niche activity highlighted in this book comes under the categories of food, fashion and accessories, and home ware. In the Random Gems chapter, interesting new formats are based around categories including bookselling and eyewear, as well as original concepts such as men's cosmetics.

The shops featured tend to be urban, relatively pricey, and have a single idea at their core. 'People in big cities have a particular fondness

Right
Powerline 6 in Hermosa
Beach, California, taps
into consumers' desire
for boutique retail
experiences.

for independents. You can't get the level of income if you are not high-end,' says Steve Collis, managing director of UK retail design group JHP, which worked on WholeMan (pages 148-51).

This is where design enters the equation. When you don't have a large marketing budget, or an existing presence (and hence profile) elsewhere, you need something to draw people into your store. Designer Mark Dytham has seen this in Japan: 'Experimental design approaches can often be found with the younger independent stores seeking to make a splash.' They're aided, he says, by their design-led and savvy approach to marketing and media, and have steadily eroded the market share of older department stores. But 'the bigger stores have started to realize the importance of design and are staging a comeback,' he says. And when niche means upmarket, the store environment must complement the products on shelf. Some store owners are responsible for the design, others bring in the professionals. Most designers love getting their teeth into an interesting start-up. 'We like it when little, one-off people with good ideas come to

us because we can do something really different, less formulaic and really experimental,' says Collis. 'For there's a strongly-held belief within the design industry that big often means samey, and small is more often innovative.'

Big chains often work with a team of marketing specialists who apply commonly used rules set out by big design firms. 'Everywhere you buy bread, coffee or sunglasses, you find the same predictable stuff that is either high-tech or nostalgic. Only small stores take risks,' says French designer Christian Biecher. Rossana Hu, store owner and designer in China (see pages 38-41 and 62-67), agrees: 'The big chain stores have to live up to a branded image that can be repeated easily and recognized without effort. This hinders too much innovation because the "tried and true" are much safer to repeat than anything experimental.'

However, designer Chris Lee (see pages 88-93) notes that in cities with high rents, it may only be the big retailers who can afford to be innovative. 'In an expensive city like London, only larger

Left
The success of small enterprises, such as the artisanal Princi bakery in Milan, has been copied by big brands.

well-established brand names have the budget to experiment with stores. Usually this is confined to flagships using "starchitects" - a classic case of retail brand endorsing architectural brand.' Examples include OMA's Prada in New York and Future Systems's flagship store for New Look in London.

While the fees for one-offs are unlikely to compare with those paid by a big client, there are at least a couple of upsides. As well as being able to push the design boundaries, the designers usually have the pleasure of dealing with a single decision maker, rather than a hierarchical institution. Or as Barcelona-based retailer Tommy Tang (see pages 28-29) puts it: 'Independent stores actually have an owner, a face, a personality, a personal direction.' Such projects are also the ones that catch the eye of the retail and design pundits and the awards judges, so the designers have a good chance of raising their profile on the back of such jobs.

As in any category of business, the big players home in on the small and quirky upstarts for ideas.

Gwen Morrison, at US retail consultancy The Store, recognizes this: 'The successes of the little shops are being adopted by the big shops.' Designer Claudio Silvestrin has direct experience of such goings-on: 'Often the image designed for a small store is replicated and copied by the big brands. The first Princi bakery I designed in Milan is a good example'. And if a start-up ends up rolling out, then the creators of the original concept may well be retained for that prize. Biecher is such an example. His concept for the French hearing store, Ecoute!Ecoute!, turned into a 12-strong chain in its first 18 months, and has plans to be 150-strong (see pages 144-47).

Of course, some of the retailers featured here have no intention of expanding. They want to maintain quality control and hope that a single outlet will become a destination in itself. Melt, an artisanal chocolate shop in London (see pages 30-33), is a case in point: 'There is a cachet in exclusivity,' believes founder Louise Nason. The Barcelona home ware retailer, Vinçon, also seems to bear this out. Others have expansion plans almost from the word go.

Below left and right
By having just one outlet, Vinçon in Barcelona has become a destination in its own right.

Maria Cousta, owner of the deli Bakaliko (see pages 16-19) already has a handful of outlets in Greece and envisages overseas shops - 'I'd like to have one in every city,' she says. David Laris, of Slice in Shanghai (see pages 38-41), is pragmatic in his reasons for expansion: 'Because of the high design and development fees, it would make more sense to do several.' Similarly, the founders of Shanghai home ware store Design Republic were planning sites in Beijing, Hangzhou, Chengdu, Shenzhen, Guangzhou, Dalian, Xiamen, Kunming and Harbin within months of opening their first outlet.

Whether these become the omnipresent chains that we're all wearying of remains to be seen. Most major players started with just one outlet. In that respect, they have become victims of their own success. As Morrison at The Store puts it, 'There is homogeneity in retail because of the popularity and success of formats like Starbucks. There was an appealing original idea at the beginning. It offered a truly different experience.' Dutch

designer Paul Linse (see pages 24-27) acknowledges this downside to expansion: 'The bigger and more global you get, the more everything is about organization and logistics, killing the original soul once so passionately created by the founder.'

There is no doubt that among the savvy and the well travelled, there is a backlash against chains. Why trek to Buenos Aires when the shops are the same as the ones you saw in Prague? As Schlosser puts it: 'The key to a successful franchise, according to many experts on the subject, can be expressed in one word: "uniformity". Franchises and chain stores strive to offer exactly the same product or service at numerous locations. Customers are drawn to familiar brands by an instinct to avoid the unknown. A brand offers reassurance when its products are always and everywhere the same.'

Brand owners who understand that their omnipresence is resulting in brand fatigue are taking drastic steps. Despite having spent years building their

Left
Ubiquitous chains
like Starbucks, which
begin as original small
businesses, can become
victims of their own
success.

brand into a household name, they are now opening outlets that pervert chain wisdom in some way – for example, a store for phone company Orange which is not called Orange and resembles a chic boutique (see pages 180-83). As Lucy Johnston, editor of GDR's Global Innovation Reports says: 'In this increasingly globalized retail market, where shopping streets are looking more and more similar, there is a growing move by many of the more adventurous brands to differentiate themselves and be more relevant to a particular locality through creating one-off retail outlets that do not conform to the typical chain approach.' Or they might try temporary venues, and like Swatch (see pages 164-69), have them decorated by graffiti artists. 'Guerrilla stores are mostly higher-end, trying to impact on the trend leaders, trying to link fashion with art,' explains Morrison.

These anti-corporate forays come under the heading of Pretenders and Guerrilla Stores, as they are either trying to look like one-offs or to look anti-chain. It's a trend we are likely to see more of as consumers turn away from our bland malls and shopping streets. 'It may not work for every brand but right now cynical consumers are so tired of marketing spin that, paradoxically, anti-big is sure to become big business,' believes Howard Saunders of consultancy Echochamber. 'Familiarity is liable to breed contempt, as Mark Twain pointed out, and that is what retail outlets must protect themselves against.'

There is no guarantee that the genuine one-off independents will last. Retail is notoriously difficult for the small player, and it may well be that some of the stores highlighted here, however aesthetically pleasing they are, may not survive until the book's publication. If that's the case, at least they have a visual legacy.

And Tom Dixon's favourite shops? They include Labour and Wait, the quirky, nostalgic kitchen and garden shop in east London, designed by its owners.

Right
Labour and Wait – a single
outlet designed by its
owners.

CHAPTER 1
FOOD

As a sector, food dominates the high-end of one-offs. Food works well in both overdeveloped and underdeveloped markets: in the former, a small food shop can offer a welcome antidote to supermarket shopping, while in the latter, an opportunity exists for speciality or high-quality products.

Joanna Blythman painted a picture of the future in her book Shopped - The Shocking Power of British Supermarkets, which could also be applied to countries following in our retail footsteps: 'If this supermarket power grab continues to go more or less unchecked, we will face a scenario where, in the not-so-distant future, most UK consumers could have no independent food shops at all but just a choice of two or three mammoth international chains and perhaps one smaller marginalized chain purveying treats and niche products to an affluent few.' This is already borne out in more developed markets. Mandy So, co-owner of Hong Kong food shop Fentons Gourmet, says that 80 per cent of the food market is occupied by several big chain stores.

Greece's modern-day grocer-cum-deli, Bakaliko, is hoping to tap into busy working mothers' lack of time for proper cooking, and urban Greeks' nostalgia for the old-fashioned local bakalikos, or grocery stores. Similarly, Boule is attempting to bring the flavour of a typical Parisian patisserie to Los Angeles and the Dutch Fishes concept is reinvigorating the dying breed of fishmongers. Meanwhile, in the developing world, upmarket one-offs are in the main aimed at globe-trotting locals or expats after something a bit more sophisticated than the neighbourhood market. Slice in Shanghai, an international deli with an emphasis on hygiene, is such a concept. And even in less mature markets, these independent retailers must battle against the supermarket onslaught. According to the researcher Mintel, in Croatia,

for example, supermarket food sales leapt from 25 per cent to 51 per cent of total food sales in the first two years of the millennium.

High prices demand sophisticated interiors and graphics, or at least that seems to be the theory. Slice, Bakaliko, Boule and Fishes all boast a strongly integrated design concept: Fishes' grey steel and glass palette was created to allow what designer Paul Linse calls 'the exclusive and very decorative fishes, which are almost like flowers' to jump out, so to speak; with its gold-framed casing, Boule's look is more jewellery store than cake shop; similarly, Bakaliko's branding wouldn't look out of place in New York's SoHo. Even environments like the chocolate shop Melt in London, which were created on a tight budget, are still expected to exude class. If there is a risk of putting off potential customers by appearing too upmarket, it's a risk that these stores seem prepared to take.

Many of these outlets also have a restaurant or café area, turning them into a destination where people can relax rather than just nip in for a quick transaction. A restaurant or some such can also boost product sales, as customers then buy the foods they've tasted. But for the sake of this book, I have focused on the retail areas.

BAKALIKO ALL THE BEST

ATHENS, GREECE
RED DESIGN CONSULTANTS

It may not be the image the rest of us like to have, but even in the kitchens of Greece people are not averse to taking culinary short cuts. The ubiquitous supermarket ready meal is yet to replace scratch cooking in Greek households but, even so, women are increasingly short of time and looking for quick, easy ways to put a meal together.

That, at least, is the understanding of Maria Cousta. 'Coming home from work (in the shipping industry), I was tired. I couldn't cook for hours to feed my family or entertain in the way I wanted. Everybody's overworked, especially mothers, so the less time they spend in the kitchen the better for them.' Her solution was a shop 'selling foodstuffs as if they were handmade'. The store, which she founded, is called Bakaliko, the generic Greek name for a local – normally family-run – grocer's, and is a modern take

on this traditional staple. Apt timing, it seems, as the original bakalikos are slowly becoming a dying breed in themselves. According to Red Design Consultants, Bakaliko's branding agency in Athens, the intense concentration of populations and financial capital, the increase in affluence, and the establishment of mass consumption, as well as the arrival of the large supermarket chains, have all had a negative impact on the more personalized and community-driven bakaliko stores.

Right
Takeaways get the brand
treatment, with the cat
character in attendance.

Τρυφερό Αγγινάρακι
σε αγνό, παρθένο
ελαιόλαδο
από την Εύβοια
€ 4,80

Above
The makeshift approach
to point- of- sale items
reinforces Bakaliko's
roots.

Right
Menu prices are chalked
up on a blackboard to
give that traditional
bakaliko touch.

- Σολωμός καπνιστός Σκωτίας
πίρι-πίρι
- Λουκάνικο Ευρυτανίας με βαλσαμ
και κρεμμύδι
- Αγκινάρες αλά Πολίτα   € 8
- Ξιφίας καπνιστός   € 9
- Σολωμός Σκωτίας με γλυκόξινη
κρεμμύδι και αυγό   € 12
- Copa di Parma   € 8
- Αυθεντικό Προσούτο Πάρμας   €1
- Κατσικίσιο τυρί Caprino €10
- Μουσακάς   € 8
- Σουπιές με σπανάκια   € 8
- Χταποδάκι κοκκινιστό   € 9
- Παραδοσιακή φακή με γιαούρτι   € 3
- Σούπα με σπαράγγια και τραχανά

Cousta's Bakaliko stocks locally made delicacies
- most of which are in own-label packaging - such as fig
preserves and meloxydo, a vinegar made from sweet wine,
honey and dried fruits. Then there are the dishes that
are made on site, to be taken away, such as potato salad
and stuffed peppers. There is also a small restaurant,
where customers can sample the fare. This, again, harks
back to the old-fashioned bakalikos which, as Rodanthi
Senduka, a partner at Red Design Consultants says, were
the heart of the neighbourhood where people went for a
gossip, an ouzo and a meze.

Cousta sources all the products herself, which has
taken her on a gastronomic journey around Greece.
'I love Greece and its Mediterranean specialities,
all its different cheeses, salamis and preserves.
For me, it's like learning about Greece all over again,
going back to our roots.'

'Bakaliko is about taking popular traditional Greek
food and making it contemporary,' says Rodanthi
Senduka. The design of Bakaliko, from interiors and
branding to packaging and in-store graphics, are the
work of Red Design Consultants. Central to the graphics
is a cat illustration - a reference to the traditional
bakalikos, which always seem to have a black cat in
attendance. This character appears on graphics and
merchandise, and is called Agapios, which is a man's
name in Greek meaning sweetheart or loved one. Other
graphics draw on the golden era of Greek television or

The trappings
of traditional
bakalikos, such as
these old scales, have
been incorporated.

old black-and-white Greek films. Inside, there is much distressed wood, and some of the furniture is covered with fabric printed with the same television graphics.

Cousta believes that she has found a gap in the market. While there are shops in Greece selling national specialities, there are none that also offer ready-made food and sandwiches. Her clientele tend to be locals and expats, and because her first two stores are in residential areas, few tourists have come across them yet. However, this relatively low profile is likely to be short-lived if Cousta's expansion plans come to fruition. Her third store, opening in the village of Porto Heli, a popular summer retreat for Athenians and yachties, will spread the message further. Her dream is to have stores in London and New York, and she has been approached about possible outlet opportunities in China. 'I'd like to have one in every city,' she says. In terms of branding and design, Bakaliko certainly looks as if it would work on an international stage. It benefits from the halo effect of the 2004 Athens Olympic Games, which has seen Greek brands better received beyond their own borders. 'Many brands have picked up on the positive climate created around the games,' says Rodanthi Senduka, and Red Design Consultants has even played on this with Bakaliko's tongue-in-cheek strapline 'since 2004'.

Below and left
Bags are illustrated with vintage Greek imagery and pictures of fresh produce, bordered with a traditional checked tablecloth motif.

BOULE

LOS ANGELES, CALIFORNIA, USA
MICHELLE MYERS

Michelle Myers had harboured a desire to open a French-style patisserie ever since she studied at Le Cordon Bleu in Paris. 'When I came back to the US I missed the neighbourhood patisseries on every corner. My dream was to one day open one in my neighborhood in LA.' This she did in 2004 with her then husband, chef David Myers. His modern French restaurant, Sona, is opposite her venture on La Cienega Boulevard, which lies between West Hollywood and Beverly Hills.

Myers describes the boulevard as 'restaurant row' - or at least that's how it was known in the late 1980s. A period of decline followed but now it's being reinvigorated with boutiques and restaurants. And that also means there are more modern, European-style cake shops springing up, but she is not fazed by the competition: 'The more the merrier, because it reinforces LA as a great food town.'

Left
The style is intended
as a loose interpretation
of Art Deco.

Right
Rather than the ornate
cases associated with
Art Deco interiors,
those at Boule are
more like the cases
in jewellery shops.

boule.

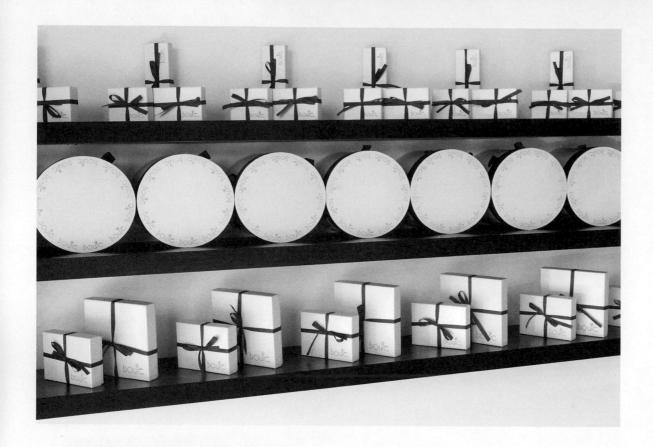

Boule's site was formerly a lighting shop selling vintage
fare from the 1950s and 1960s. It is named after a specific
round, artisan French loaf, and Myers hopes to introduce
a bread offer at some point. Meanwhile, Boule has built
up a reputation for sourcing local, seasonal ingredients
from places like the Santa Monica Farmers' Market and San
Diego's Chino Farms. The shop's range includes chocolate,
conserves, ice cream and pastries – from jasmine tea-honey
and Sicilian pistachio madeleines to cranberry-walnut
biscotti.

While Myers started out with an architect to create the
store, she says, 'We didn't get along and they pulled out
halfway through. So it's my design. I wanted something
that reflected my philosophy of cuisine; my technique is
a modern take on classical French.' She describes the
design as taking the traditional Art Deco patisserie and
modernizing it. 'Traditional shops have ornate gold-
detailed casings in rounded marble. My casings are more
sleek and linear, so that they are more like jewellery
cases. In fact, it became more like a jewellery store.'

The materials used mix sophistication with an industrial feel: lots of dark wood and a floor of poured concrete, along with metal trays for the cases. The shelving is also dark wood, and carries neat, pyramidal piles of cake boxes tied up with wide brown ribbon. Meanwhile, sweets are displayed in traditional round glass jars. Myers describes the graphics, which she also designed, as having the same sleek, sophisticated feel. And the narrow, lower-case letters hark back to the Art Deco era.

The intention is to open two more Boules in the LA area. Unlike some owners of handmade food outlets, she has no qualms that her service or offer would suffer with expansion. 'It's about how strong your management team, training and company culture is.'

Opposite
The dark wood shelves carry aesthetically stacked packaging.

Left
Boule's sleek logo appears on all boxes, which are finished off with a wide brown ribbon.

FISHES

UTRECHT AND AMSTERDAM
THE NETHERLANDS
STUDIO LINSE

Specialist food shops like bakers, butchers and fishmongers
have been hard hit by the relentless onslaught of the big
supermarkets. Indeed, in Amsterdam, the number of fishmongers
fell by 30 per cent in five years, according to Bart van Olphen.
But despite, or because of, this sad state of affairs he
spotted an opportunity. And he's had a fair bit of catering
experience to marry with his scheme. A graduate of The Hague's
Hotelschool, van Olphen worked as a chef in several Michelin-
starred restaurants, and started a high-class catering
company in Budapest. In 1999, he set up the operations for
Vakzuid, a club and restaurant in Amsterdam. 'Here I started to
learn about global cuisine and the role of fish in the different
kitchen styles,' he says. 'My job included analyzing the menu
items sold every evening, and I concluded that fish was the most
sold.' Interestingly, the best-selling fish was not stocked
in quality Amsterdam fishmongers. What's more, his market
research showed that consumers did not know how to cook fish
at home. Hence his idea for a new-style fishmonger: high-
quality fish (mostly from sustainable fisheries) sold by
experienced cooks in a modern and clean environment.

Above
At Fishes, the simple
display allows the
high-quality product
to speak for itself.

Right
Studio Linse
accentuated the long,
narrow space with
a similarly shaped
counter.

To do this idea justice, Amsterdam's Studio Linse has gone to town. 'Our starting point was to make an architectural base that would make the beautiful product stand out,' explains the studio's Paul Linse. The colour palette is just two shades of grey, which is complemented by plain glass and polished stainless steel. The walls and floor are both cast resin. 'The fish they sell is exclusive and very decorative, almost like flowers, and we put them in a surrounding that doesn't "affect" them', Linse explains. The first outlet, in Utrechtsestraat, is narrow and long, more a corridor than a room. 'Instead of trying to hide that fact, we emphasized it by using linear counters and, at the far back of the store, a mirrored wall,' he adds.

At the moment there are four Fishes in The Netherlands: two in Amsterdam, one in Laren and one in Utrecht. The first Belgian store, near Ghent, opened in February 2007, and other outlets in Brussels and Antwerp, as well as Haarlem and The Hague in The Netherlands, are also being planned.

0   2.5   5m
   7.5   15ft

Above
Walls and floors are of durable cast resin.

Left
Plan. The entrance is to the right with the long display case running down the centre, and the 'larder' to the left.

Right
The grey colour
palette allows
the colours of the
seafood to sing.

Below right
Complementary wines
and other products are
displayed in a larder-
like area at the back
of the store.

Left and below
Papabubble's Barcelona
outlet maintained the
original shopfront
and floor.

PAPABUBBLE

BARCELONA, SPAIN, AMSTERDAM,
THE NETHERLANDS, TOKYO, JAPAN
TOMMY TANG AND CHRIS KING

An owner-designed format, Papabubble is a twenty-first-century sweet shop. The handmade goodies range from lollypops, edible rings and organic candies to a bespoke service of sculptures for the corporate and wedding markets.

Papabubble was the idea of Tommy Tang, who has a family history of hotels and small businesses. He was joined by fellow Australian, Chris King, an industrial designer by training. But rather than launching Papabubble at home, they set sail for Europe. 'Australia is a great place to start, learn and test your skills and brand power, but it is reasonably easy to reach the top of your field there,' Tang explains. 'We thought by moving to Europe, where there is a very long history of artisania, we would find more inspiration and a more diverse market.'

Papabubble launched in Barcelona in 2003, with Amsterdam and Tokyo following in 2005. The duo is now scouting New York, Seoul and Istanbul for further sites.

Right and far right
The highly styled
confectionery acts
as the store's interior
decoration.

Bottom right
The brightly coloured
sweets are manufactured
by hand.

Below
King invites artists
to create illustrations
for his packaging.

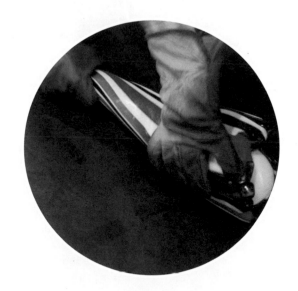

In terms of location, they know where they don't want to be:
shopping centres, shopping streets and high-end shopping areas.
'We generally like our customers to have to seek us out, though
not too far. We look for character buildings with reasonable
rentals that are handy for public transport, and
if there are lots of trees, even better!' says Tang.

So the Barcelona store is located in a 200-year-old palace,
whose previous tenants – the same family for 132 years – were
also artisans, though their chosen materials were metal and
lead. In those days there was a factory on site and a retail
space at the front. 'We like to respect the actual building and
its tradition, so in Barcelona we have retained all the original
floors, shopfront and ceilings, while creating a contrast with
our very designed packaging and display areas,' says Tang.

The sweets themselves are like multicoloured jewels, and
would stand out in the blandest of interiors. The graphics,
courtesy of King, manage to strike a balance between childlike
fun and adult stylishness. While King has creative control,
he occasionally invites various artists to come up with specific
illustrations for the brand.

MELT

Many in the industry talk about the theatre of retail. This can often mean concocting some sort of interactive element to engage your customers with a particular product, such as wine tasting or a demonstration of some gadget or other. Your cause is helped if your stock has something genuinely theatrical about it, and this is where food outlets win hands down. Ever since the humble pizza oven, customers have been drawn in by real live cooking – even more so these days, when hardly anyone can remember how to prepare food from scratch. At Melt, the theatre is supplied through the art of making chocolate, for this is an artisanal chocolate shop of the highest order.

Architects Michaelis Boyd had a limited budget, meaning little of the site could be changed structurally. However, they did manage to open up the kitchen area at the back of the small space so that the culinary activity could be seen from the street. And if that doesn't draw people in, the rich aroma will.

Left
The scent of
chocolate lures
passers-by in from
the street.

This page
The inside is simple
bordering on stark,
enlivened only by a
couple of vintage
chandeliers and the
product itself.

By keeping the interiors as minimal as possible, the stock gets to sing. Little, carefully compiled piles of confectionery are arranged along a back-lit, white marble shelf. In fact, everything is white, except the brown poured resin floor. 'We kept it simple and utilitarian,' says Alex Michaelis of Michaelis Boyd. 'Most chocolate shops are very intricate and you can't see the product.' All this stark simplicity is offset by a couple of large antique chandeliers, chosen by the owner Louise Nason.

A shop selling handmade chocolate at around £9.80 per 100 grams ($18 per 16 ounces) is not going to find a market everywhere, but Nason has confidence in the locale and in her clientele. 'I live near here and identified with my clients, and so I fit the shop around them,' she says. The site is on chichi Ledbury Road in Notting Hill – a street peppered with boutiques. It's not unusual to find chocolate alongside fashion, she adds, as it's another luxury product. The site is at the north end of the road, which was known as 'Deadbury Road' for its fast turnover of failed enterprises. But Melt is hoping to buck that trend, and Nason has already got a lot of regular clients. Indeed, at the time of going to press the upmarket fashion chain Reiss had just opened a store opposite, while designer shoe boutique Iris opened next door.

It was Nason, who worked at the auction house Christie's before she had her children, who came up with the name.

'It describes the correct way to taste chocolate. And it's an oozy "love" word which you're unlikely to forget.' Plus, she suggests, it even lends itself to subliminal advertising every time you read it in a recipe.

The element of theatre extends from the kitchen to the curved counter at the front of the shop. Each chocolate is wrapped in unbleached paper, and popped in simple brown and white boxes. These are then tied with a coloured ribbon, sourced by Nason from a man in Bethnal Green who supplies the rag trade. For Nason, 'It's about making an effort and being generous. I never rush people when they come into the shop.' In terms of direct competition, it seems there isn't any nearby. Hotel Chocolat is in the neighbourhood but it is part of a chain.

Even if this store, which opened in 2006, becomes a long-term roaring success, Nason has no plans to roll out the Melt concept. 'It's not my intention to have a chain,' she says, believing that any more would dilute the original offer. Her role models are other single-site enterprises, and she credits the success of the high-profile London restaurant, River Café, to firmly sticking to just one outlet. 'People are prepared to travel there. There is a cachet in exclusivity.'

Opposite top
The open kitchen can be seen at the back of the shop.

Opposite bottom
The shelving is simple marble, showing off the premium chocolates to good effect.

Left and far left
Melt's carefully sourced packaging reflects the quality of both the shop's interior and the chocolate itself.

FENTONS GOURMET

HONG KONG, CHINA, DERRICK TSANG

Fentons Gourmet is a one-off with a design innovation that's drawing the crowds. The international food emporium is the creation of Derrick Tsang, and it's his folding timber screen door that is attracting all the attention. The tall, west-facing façade gave Tsang the opportunity to create the device. He describes it as a pronounced timber screen in front of the glass shop windows which acts as a shade against the intense, western sunlight and hence against the heat. 'Filter shadows become ephemeral patterns and mark the passing of time like a sundial,' he says. 'During business hours, a section of the screen folds up to reveal the glass sliding entrance door and is transformed into a projected beak-shaped entrance canopy. At night when the shop closes, it folds back down and retracts like a shutter.'

Fentons opened in Happy Valley, a residential quarter of Hong Kong, in 2005. It's aimed at well-heeled foodies, with such delights on offer as lavender and lemon salts, handmade pasta from Italy and a butcher with seasonal meats. And being in Happy Valley, it's well-positioned for its target market as it rubs shoulders with a host of private clubs, including the Jockey Club and the Cricket Club.

Fentons is the brainchild of two couples, all of whom studied in North America. Co-founder Mandy So describes them as having backgrounds in finance and manufacturing. 'Being passionate about food, the concept seemed the right fit for all of us,' she says.

Inside, the space is divided into retail, sales and preparation areas. 'High ceilings over the retail and sales areas are separately roofed over by a folding timber skin and a perforated, cheese-like cover respectively,' explains Tsang. These conceal all the building services in the ceiling void and provide an undulated volume for the overhead sign boxes and the hanging LCD monitor. 'I treated it like designing a boutique hotel, so much of the rest of the built-in items and loose furniture are custom-made to add richness and features to the shop.'

With the assistance of the graphic designer Lau Kwok-Fai, Tsang has provided a one-stop design service for the founders, from designing the company logo, shopping bags and wrapping papers, to the price tags, uniforms and delivery van graphics. 'I was hoping that something different would catch people's attention and make an unforgettable experience,' Tsang says.

Opposite
The vertical slatted façade carries Fentons' elegant lower-case logo.

Far left
The retail area sits at the front of the shop.

Above
During the day, the slats cast shadows over the interior and help keep the heat out.

Right
Tsang's folding slatted door in action.

GOŬ

BEIRUT, LEBANON, MARINA YOUNAN

'We were always frustrated not to find innovative food
products in the Middle East' was the starting point for
Ossama el Kaoukji and his two partners, Patricia Kebbe
and Nicha Sursock, for the creation of Goŭ . The founders
had a background in marketing and food management: Kebbe
and el Kaoukji had worked in advertising, and Sursock had
set up a number of fashionable restaurants in Cairo. All
three wanted to bring imaginative foods and dishes in
good-looking packaging to Lebanon.

The first store, which opened at the beginning of 2006,
is in the heart of Ashrafieh, an affluent yet hip quarter
of Beirut. 'On its shopping streets designer boutiques
border art galleries, and outdoor cafés sit beside
retail shops along tree-lined sidewalks, making the
district a fashionable residential spot, a prime
commercial location, and the most desirable food and
entertainment destination,' says Kebbe. The three
partners see themselves as trendsetters of taste. 'We
look for the hottest products from around the world with
exotic flavours and innovative packaging designs, and
are the first to introduce them to the Middle Eastern
markets. We're after food "collections", which change
with the flow of seasons and conjure a novel experience,
a culinary excursion, or a sensory revelation. Goŭ , to

some extent, is the Colette of food,' she adds, referring to the Parisian home ware store.

Goŭ 's stock is certainly novel: red rice from Bhutan, Tibetan Monks' 'secret tea', Peruvian Inca Inchi oil, strawberry, mint and pepper jam, comfit of lavender and jasmine, and dark chocolate with wasabi, ginger and sesame seeds. It is never going to replace the grocery store, but that's not its aim, as Kebbe states: 'We are more about a fashionable food boutique than an ordinary deli shop.' For Goŭ is where fashion and food collide, hence the runaway success of the Swarovski crystal-covered water bottles and the edible candy rings.

Judging by the buzz around Ashrafieh, Goŭ seems to be in the right place at the right time. 'Beirut has recently become very conscious of the added value that smart and innovative architecture and design can contribute to the retail business growth,' explains Kebbe. 'Retail's most dynamic sectors – food and fashion – have clearly taken the lead in Beirut's vibrant downtown area and in Ashrafieh. We can see an increasing number of casual and themed restaurants, small hotels and fashion boutiques setting new design standards.'

The enthusiasm with which Goŭ 's founders have embraced the idea of creating a retail brand is best expressed in its positioning statement: 'Like the graceful flight of an enchanting butterfly in a field of bloom, Goŭ glides your senses over a tempting garden of gourmet delights.' It perhaps loses something in translation.

While Goŭ 's design execution was carried out by local architect Marina Younan, the founders credit themselves with the concept. The aim was to create an open store, based on a cost-effective, modifiable and durable display system. Because Goŭ outlets will always be located in the main hall areas of upmarket shopping malls – close to fashion and jewellery boutiques – the structure was designed in a square format with all four sides open to public access. All its elements (wood, Corian, crystal, stainless steel and built-in lighting) were designed in such a modular way that the store size can be adapted to any layout of future units. What's more, the whole flat-pack system can be dismantled and stored in custom-made wooden boxes, to allow for eventual shipping to overseas markets. In October 2006, the owners were eyeing-up sites in Kuwait, Dubai and Cairo. The intention for 2007 and beyond was to open in Japan and the US.

SLICE

SHANGHAI, CHINA, NERI & HU DESIGN
AND RESEARCH OFFICE

David Laris, a former executive chef of London's Mezzo,
moved to China in 2003 to open a restaurant. In the
research and development stage of Laris Restaurant
he discovered what a challenge it was to source good-
quality foods there. 'I saw a huge gap in the market,'
he says. And as he was researching all these foods and
meeting suppliers, 'it made sense to develop a retail
concept to bring more products into the country and
then use them in the restaurant'. Slice (as in slice
of life), a fledgling chain of upmarket, international
delis, was the result, with the first outlet opening
in 2006 in the Shanghai suburb of Qingpu. 'It's a
fairly wealthy, up-scale neighbourhood,' says Slice's
designer, Lyndon Neri of Shanghai-based Neri & Hu
Design and Research Office (NHDRO).

This is a truly gourmet destination boasting Roquefort,
Stilton and Manchego cheeses, Serrano and Parma
hams, foie gras, Ferrigno sardines, San Pellegrino
beverages, La Perruche cane sugars, wines by Penfolds,
and champagnes by Dom Perignon and Veuve Clicquot.
So Slice is - initially at least - aimed at expats and
returnees. However, its eventual goal is to attract
locals with a taste for good-quality, healthy and
fresh produce. 'There is a fast-growing interest and
awareness among the middle-class Chinese community
about this sort of thing. This fascination with world
food and increased exposure will further draw them
to this sort of concept,' believes Laris. Hence,
everything in the stores is bilingual (English and
Mandarin), and Slice stocks top-notch Asian products
as well as Western items.

NHDRO sees Slice as bridging the gulf between the old
world street markets, which were lined with fresh
produce and created an experience for the shopper, and
the new world supermarkets, where technology and design
has turned the experience into a practice in efficiency.
'In a modern world that has devalued human experience,
our design captures the spirit of the marketplace in
creating a human-centred experience,' says Neri.

Above
The reception area
incorporates a traditional
Chinese screen motif which
filters natural light and
creates patterns across
the floor.

Left
Except for the doors
displaying the store logo,
the entrance, in front of
a reflective pool, is glass
to allow a view of the
merchandise inside.

The space is divided into three rooms: a central cashier, a marketplace and a deli. 'The central area is also where you enter and it is surrounded by wooden screens that filter natural light creating depth, a sense of scale and patterns across the floor,' says Neri. 'These screens are an integral part of Chinese domestic spaces,' she adds, 'and the concept clearly draws on the country's traditional design aesthetic.' The 'market' is flanked by tables and chairs, creating a figurative city street – what Neri calls a modern abstraction of an old world market. Meanwhile, the deli area is covered in a canopy, 'reinforcing a sense of domesticity and warmth that is conveyed throughout the design,' Neri adds.

Laris takes provenance and authenticity seriously. This can be seen by the in-store collateral, which explains where items come from, how they were selected and how they should be best used. Hence, Slice's tastings and demonstrations: 'It's our strong desire to connect with the customer, to build a relationship and be their local grocer – so to speak – while still drawing on an international knowledge of food and professional service.' He admits that none of this will be achieved overnight in China and expects to make a decent return in year two or three.

While Slice has no direct competition at present, Laris acknowledges that this will quickly change. When others realize that the gap between mass and boutique can be filled with a solid concept, then 'we expect to see real competitors emerging in this area of the market'.

The second, third and fourth Slices are due to open within a year of the first in the city centre. Laris's expansion plans are bullish, to say the least. He envisages around 20 Slices of two different formats around China, with a further four in other Southeast Asian countries, all within the next five years.

Above
Displays continue the graphic theme, with food items grouped by taste and texture.

40

TENDER   SPICY

Above
Dark wood cabinetry
allows the brightly
coloured food
packaging to stand
out, while deli table
tops are the same
marble as used for the
reception desk.

Above right
This tea cabinet
recalls traditional
Chinese shop fittings.

Right
NHDRO's identity and
packaging for Slice
is consistently simple.

Above
Princi's second outlet,
on via Speronari, has an
un-baker-like façade.

Right
The long bronze counter
is flanked by a textured
wall inset with a niche
for seven candles.

PRINCI

MILAN, ITALY
CLAUDIO SILVESTRIN ARCHITECTS

For anyone used to the ubiquitous, low-end bakery chains
such as Greggs in the UK, Princi will come as something
of a culture shock. Like London chocolate shop Melt (see
pages 30-33), Princi is all about the theatre of retail.
In this case the chefs - kitted out in Giorgio Armani
uniforms - are creating breads and pastas.

Princi is the brainchild of entrepreneur Rocco Princi,
who has been dubbed the Armani of bread - making those
uniforms even more apt. South Calabrian-born Mr Princi
moved to Milan in the 1980s, and is a well-known character
there. He has a handful of Princi outlets, only two
of which have so far received the Claudio Silvestrin
treatment.

This second 'designed' Princi opened in via Speronari,
just off the Duomo, in 2006, and although it uses slightly
different materials and has a different layout from the
first Silvestrin Princi (see page 10), the interiors of the
two shops are very much in the same vein.

The architects have taken as their theme the very stuff of life. Hence the elements that go into making bread – water, air, earth and fire – are all present or suggested. As Silvestrin says of the first outlet: 'The materials I chose are an unusual mixture of colours: brass panels in a scorched-earth tone for the main desk and walls, slabs of smooth porphyry in a grey/violet tone for the floor and rough porphyry for the dwarf wall.' In this new store, the porphyry marble is white.

Silvestrin was keen to create a tension between, as he describes it, 'the warm tones of materials and the sharp, but sensual geometrical drawing. This shop stands out as a new embodiment of thinking about a bakery without any distinction between the laboratory and the shopping area. Hence the new "theatrical" image, with both clientele and bakers as main characters on the same stage'. Both outlets have a glass wall, which separates customers from the art – and heat – of baking.

Other eye-catching features on via Speronari include a stretched 19 metre (62 foot) long bronze counter with a rough porphyry lending texture to the wall behind. 'The mighty impact of this earth-wall is softened by the gentle features of a waterfall and by seven candles, which are placed inside the wall,' says Silvestrin. Meanwhile, recessed ceiling spotlights concentrate their focus on the bread and only the bread.

Princis are open 24 hours a day, and peckish or parched Milanese can nip in not just for a pastry but for a coffee, too.

At the moment, these two Princis stand out in Milan. 'There are no other high-design bakeries here,' says Massimo Deconti, architect at Claudio Silvestrin.

Above
The three-dimensional
window display device
is designed to intrigue
passers-by.

Right
Plan
1 Retail
2 Workshop
3 Brick oven
4 WC

Far right
Armani-clad artisans
are all part of Princi's
theatre.

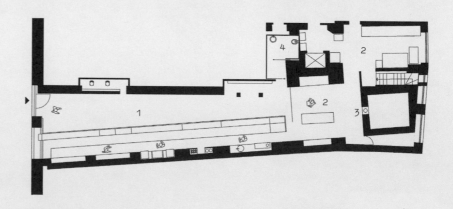

Chapter 2
Home
and Lifestyle

Home and lifestyle stores indulge the desire of modern home owners and renters to get the look, live the brand and, in general, aspire. One has the impression that many such shops are taking their inspiration from such long-running success stories as Colette in Paris. Some, like Mercado Moderno, are conventional home ware stores; others, such as Isolée are better described as lifestyle destinations.

Unsurprisingly, it is in this category that I have come across the most designer-owners – either real-life designers who like the idea of having a platform to indulge their own taste in furnishing, or the entrepreneur-turned-interior designer. For example, the founders of Neri & Hu Design and Research Office in Shanghai are also the founders of the Chinese retail venture Design Republic, and they certainly seem to have gone to town on the finishes. At the more modest end of the scale One, in Oslo, is on the ground floor of Bleed Design's studio and is simple, bordering on basic. And Mercado Moderno's bricolage feel is intentional as its owners Marcelo Vasconcellos and Alberto Vicente wanted to preserve the old Rio building's original characteristics. Similarly, Jonas Ericsson is the sole creator of his Scandinavian forest, Style:Nordic, in its unlikely location of downtown Singapore. Others, like Isolée in Madrid and San Francisco's Friend, turned to the professionals, in the shape of Teresa Sapey and fuseproject respectively.

These hybrid environments are very much intended to reflect not only the taste of their founders, but their founders' interpretation of a covetable lifestyle. Hence, most offer products for sale alongside a café of some sort. This is certainly the case for Garage in Riga, Isolée and Artgadgets in Eindhoven.

While some promise to bring international design names and products to a new market, others trumpet local talent. It depends where these retailers have seen the gap in their market, and where their own aspirations lie. Either way, their intention is to offer a well-edited product range. This helps to differentiate them from department stores and home ware chains such as Target in the US and the UK's Habitat.

In design terms, these outlets must find a balance between an aspirational environment and one which champions the products. In general, the look is minimal or at least pared back.

For most founders, these are genuine one-offs, and they have no intention of re-creating them elsewhere. Only Design Republic's owners have their sights set on immediate and rapid expansion.

Isolée

MADRID, SPAIN
TERESA SAPEY
ARCHITECTURE STUDIO

When Isoleé opened in 2005, it was a one-off for
Spain's capital, incorporating, as it does, a number
of activities. Suddenly, Madrileños had somewhere to
go for the latest Japanese designer shirt, a retro-
modern Italian lamp and a spot of lunch. The store's
strapline is fashion + food + lifestyle, and its
two floors are split into a cafeteria, retail area
delicatessen and lounge. Because this is all about
an aspirational lifestyle, the café serves teas from
the Himalayas and imported beverages from the US
and Japan; the deli stocks food from five continents,
including sushi and Mexican delicacies; and the home
ware section includes modern furniture classics from
Driade and Artemide.

Main image
The graphic tree motif, which appears on the ground-floor window, was created by designer Teresa Sapey to wind its branches around the store.

Inset
The tree, which can also be seen from outside, shows off Isolée's strong corner position in Madrid's chichi Chueca district.

The task of creating a coherent whole from these elements was handed to Madrid-based Teresa Sapey Architecture Studio. Sapey's starting point was a tree on a wall on the ground floor with its branches extending out in an orderly sprawl into all areas. Hues of grey decorate the walls on both floors in parallel lines, 'and in order to differentiate Isoleé's various functions, the store's flooring is wood, and the bar's flooring is black ceramic,' Sapey explains. For the store's own furniture, Sapey has combined pieces from well-known manufacturers (such as Foscarini's bar lamps) with her studio's own designs, which include the red and white leather cubes.

Isoleé is located in Madrid's trendy Chueca district, just off Gran Via. But rather than resting on their retail laurels, the founders - two young, well-travelled Spaniards, José Luis Robles and Rodrigo Menendez - are sizing up other European capitals to see if they can replicate their success in Madrid.

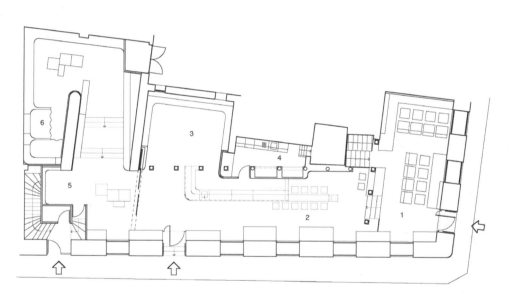

Ground-floor plan
1 Entrance
2 Bar
3 Delicatessen
4 Kitchen
5 Retail store
6 Fitting room

Left
The outlet's various
functions are
differentiated by the
choice of flooring.

Below
The tree's branches
even make their way
onto this glass wall
in the toilets.

The 500 square metre (5,380 square foot) space, which is open from 10:30am to 11pm, includes a café-lounge complete with futuristic refreshment cabinets.

Style:Nordic

SINGAPORE, JONAS ERICSSON

Birch logs not only make a place look Scandinavian, but, according to natives of that region, they make it smell Scandinavian. This suits Jonas Ericsson who opened his lifestyle store Style:Nordic in 2005. Ericsson chose Singapore as his location, having researched its retail scene during his International Business and Economics MSc. 'During my semester of studies here, I found that Singapore was lacking Scandinavian design. I saw an opportunity to set up a company that promoted and sold the famous designer products in a lifestyle concept.'

The shop is located on Ann Siang Hill, which Ericsson describes as the heart of Singapore. 'It's an old part of Chinatown with old shop-houses, some of which have been renovated and some not,' he says, and, in fact, he is the first retail tenant of his 1926 building.

'The crowd here is very mixed with both old Chinese associations, or clans, as they are called, and chic restaurants, and now also some stores that put their emphasis on design,' he explains. 'It is called a hip area of Singapore since there are a lot of advertising agencies, design companies and architects in the neighbourhood. I would say it is a cutting edge, upcoming area for shopping.' His intention is to attract both private and corporate clients.

Left
The clothes racks by David Design, seen here just inside the entrance, are easily relocated.

Above
Corporate clients are taken to the more serene surroundings of the first floor.

Main Picture
The lighting is
intended to suggest
daylight.

Ericsson, whose previous job was as a manager for Giorgio Armani Sweden, has set out to introduce Scandinavian modern classics to the Singaporean market. As a lifestyle store, Style:Nordic stocks fashion, home accessories, furniture and furnishings such as carpets, lighting, wallpaper and fabrics from big name designers such as Alvar Aalto, Johannes Norlander and Eero Koivisto. 'The doors are always open and everybody should feel welcome. This, I feel, is important, since the products are new to Singapore and people are curious to see and touch them. A friendly atmosphere is also very important since the prices are quite high by Singaporean standards.'

Style:Nordic is on two 120 square metre (1,292 square foot) floors. The shop layout downstairs is busier, more funky and with louder music (Scandinavian, of course) than upstairs, where a calmer showroom

Below left and right
Downstairs the simple shelving contains displays of Scandinavian tableware, stationery and gifts.

Right
A Nordic pastoral scene was created to display the outdoor furniture.

56

offers design consultation, and where the products are displayed in a more domestic environment.

Ericsson, who also created the logo, says of the interior design: ' It is supposed to be very Scandinavian - simple with no fuss and easy to understand. I knew the "story" I wanted to tell when I opened the store, about how a tree looks before it is cut down and turned into furniture. This is the story of the blond Scandinavian style and its forest heritage. I also wanted to show contemporary design in an old Singaporean shop- house so the customer can see that they work well together. ' With this in mind he placed the forest downstairs. A photo- wooded wallpaper, a lawn- like carpet, and birch logs all the way from Sweden created the effect he was after.

The carpet is used to display outdoor furniture from Nola, cushions and picnic equipment. And Ericsson has used some furniture to good effect as part of the store's own environment. Hence the String Shelf designed in 1949 by Nils Strinning. The gables are painted white, and the rest of the shelves are either painted white or birch. Both the shelves and gables are ' open' so customers can see all the way across the interior. The lighting is bright but in a daylight way, Ericsson adds, rather than giving the feeling of an Indian restaurant.

One

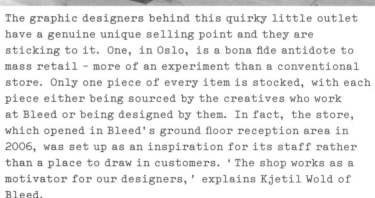

™ BUY
ONE
ITS
GONE

Above
The shop's logo is
constructed around the
numeral 1.

Top left, top right
and opposite
The shop also hosts
installations by
artists, clients and the
designers themselves.

The graphic designers behind this quirky little outlet
have a genuine unique selling point and they are
sticking to it. One, in Oslo, is a bona fide antidote to
mass retail – more of an experiment than a conventional
store. Only one piece of every item is stocked, with each
piece either being sourced by the creatives who work
at Bleed or being designed by them. In fact, the store,
which opened in Bleed's ground floor reception area in
2006, was set up as an inspiration for its staff rather
than a place to draw in customers. 'The shop works as a
motivator for our designers,' explains Kjetil Wold of
Bleed.

Being graphic designers, it is no surprise that the
store's identity comes complete with its own well-honed
raison d'être. The logo is built around the number one,
with each letter comprising that digit. The environment
itself is simple, bordering on stark. 'We have clean
white surfaces which allow the products to shine with
their unique qualities. The surfaces are also made
that way so we can put in any concept we like and it
still doesn't affect the actual event,' Wold explains;
One hosts installations and exhibitions by artists,
clients or even Bleed designers themselves. However,
they have gone to town with a fancy merchandising unit.
This comes in the shape of what Wold describes as 'the
amazing Alu rail system' and is intended to give the shop
an international look and feel.

The sorts of individual item that One's customers might pick up include a specially designed dress from Norwegian designer T-Michael, books from Japan, Alta city bikes, designer toys, a lamp from Swedish designers Konkret Form, as well as work from Arne&Carlos, Johan Verde and Rune Johansen. Work by international designers such as Junko Mizuno, Marc Jacobs, James Jarvis, Colette Paris, Krv Kurva, Linda Isola, Jasper Morrison, Juan Durval and Jean Sebastian Ides are also to be found. Being stocked completely with one-offs, the onus is on the customer to make that purchase, for fear of never being able to find the item easily again. One's founders are realistic, though, about the store's commercial potential. 'We earn just enough to pay our expenses,' explains Wold. 'The main purpose is not to make money – it would be impossible in Oslo, as it's a small market for independent stores focusing on design. Our goal is to present desirable products and be a launch pad for new and exclusive products or artists.'

This experiment is in good company. One, and hence Bleed Design, are located at Grünerløkka Trondheimsveien 2 in an old brewery. This pretty area is home to a host of independent stores, galleries, cafés and art students. One is aimed at 'people looking for the experience you don't find in any of the large chain stores,' says Wold. And just to stress its distinctness from the chains' extended opening times, One is only open one day a week on a Thursday. Its motto is: 'closed almost every day'.

Top and left
Each individual piece of stock is hand-picked by Bleed's designers, and all are displayed on clean, white surfaces.

Right
Clothes are hung on simple movable rails, allowing maximum flexibility.

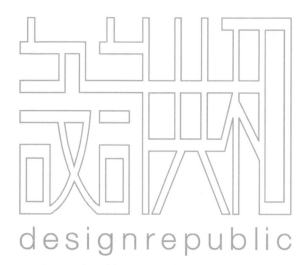

Design Republic

SHANGHAI, CHINA
NERI & HU DESIGN AND RESEARCH OFFICE

When it comes to decision-making around a new store concept, it helps if you are the owners as well as the designers. Design Republic's founders, Lyndon Neri and Rossana Hu, double as the founding partners of Neri & Hu Design and Research Office (NHDRO). Both members of the Chinese diaspora, they have returned to their homeland after studying and working in the US. They spotted a gap in the market when they came to Shanghai from the US to oversee the construction of another retail scheme. 'During that year of living and working here, we saw that although Shanghai was booming economically, there was a design vacuum,' says Hu. 'There is a real need to raise the design consciousness of society as a whole, and so setting up Design Republic as a "platform for design" was the initial intention. This is to be a place where design excellence can be exhibited, sold, enjoyed, discussed and learned.'

The Bund in Shanghai, where the store opened in 2005, is what Neri describes as the city's most significant historic district, and possibly the most prime commercial real estate strip in China. 'From 2003 to 2006, this district changed from a tourist spot to the most sought after high-end retail and restaurant district,' continues Neri. 'It is still considered "up and coming", since only a few buildings have been fully renovated, but the brands that have moved in are well-established international fashion giants such as Zegna, Armani and D&G. Currently, the district is still a mix of down and dirty local joints with world class glamour houses.'

62

Above
The owners, who are
also designers, were
responsible for the
shop's graphics and
packaging.

Top
The store was designed
not to have a
conventional retail
look.

Pieces by many of the big international names of today and yesterday are to be found at Design Republic's maiden site, including Eileen Gray, Jean Prouvé, Charles and Ray Eames, Arne Jacobsen and Marcel Wanders. Many of these products had never before been available to consumers in China, the duo claims. There are also Neri- and Hu- designed items, under their brand Design Republic.

In terms of the look, the pair were after what they call a fresh shopping experience. 'We explored a more raw approach to materials and took a chance on an aesthetic that is not so conventionally "retail",' says Neri. The environment is intended to act as a backdrop on which the products are displayed. 'To be a blank canvas, the store had to exist quietly, yet exude strong taste and character,' says Hu. Hence the basic materials of concrete, brushed bronze, strips of solid oak panels, and raw steel. 'They are all used in their natural finishes, with almost no protective coating, finished with a sanding or brushed technique, rather than being painted or varnished. Not only is the natural beauty revealed in these materials, they become a contrast to the refined products in- store,' Hu adds.

Left
The materials used were left in their natural state.

Right
Glass panels can be drawn completely to surround the central area.

Bottom right
Iconic pieces from past and present are given a museum-like display.

Meanwhile, floor-to-ceiling glass panels are positioned to be very flexible. 'In moments they become doors, leading to display shelves, the reception table or the entry lobby. When the central space is surrounded completely by these glass panels, the experience is like window shopping, only now the customer is inside the store instead of outside,' says Neri.

And finally, Design Republic has a central platform in wood and sheet metal, which its owners hope will act as a literal platform for the domestic and international design community. 'This should be a place where the best designs in the world are showcased in Shanghai, and the design community can use it as a platform to exchange ideas, draw inspiration and make selections for clients,' says Hu. The idea is to put on small-scale exhibitions. 'On this platform, Design Republic hopes not only to sell high-quality products, but to lift the bar in the design world to help nurture new interests in design,' she adds.

The intention is for the brand to quickly become a China-wide chain, with sites mooted in nine other cities.

Right
The platform zone is intended to act as an exhibition space.

Below
The solid oak flooring brings warmth to what is otherwise a fairly minimalist space.

66

Above
The store is located
in a previously
derelict 1912
building.

Top left, below
and right
The shop's exposed
brickwork, which was
originally criticized,
was at the forefront
of the trend for
deconstructivism.

Mercado Moderno

RIO DE JANEIRO, BRAZIL
MARCELLO VASCONCELLOS
AND ALBERTO VICENTE

Rua do Lavradio, in the old Lapa district of Rio, has
created a name for itself as a mecca for vintage design.
The street is full of such stores but this hasn't
dissuaded Marcelo Vasconcellos and Alberto Vicente,
both art dealers who had previously handled vintage
design. They believe that their enterprise, Mercado
Moderno, offers Lapa's shoppers something different.
Along with 1950s to 1980s Brazilian furniture from
designers such as Tenreiro, Sérgio Rodrigues,
Zanini and Zalzupin, they also stock international
pieces. Unsurprisingly, Mercado Moderno's customers
– architects, interior designers, collectors and
design enthusiasts – are more than happy to come here.
For along with all the antique emporia and colonial
architecture, Lapa, with its buzzy nightlife, is known
as the Montmartre of the Tropics.

The store is in a previously abandoned 1912 building. The two owners took on the roles of architects as well as engineers and decorators, setting out to conserve its historical look. They rebuilt the upper floor with timber from a colonial farm within Brazil's interior and left the bricks exposed, to give the store what Vasconcellos calls a modern and warm atmosphere. They were criticized for the brickwork at first, as people felt it would overwhelm the products, but then deconstructivism became popular, and the bricks were accepted.

Mercado Moderno has the look of a pleasantly higgledy-piggledy junk shop (which no doubt belies the prices). Its long, narrow room – an almost church-like space – is lit by high wall lights. Further illumination is provided by table and standing lamps, which are also for sale.

The store, which opened in 2003, is a success but there are no plans to open any further outlets as the one-off nature of the products simply doesn't lend itself to that. 'We deal with unique design objects so there wouldn't be enough copies or equals to supply a chain,' says Vasconcellos.

Above and far left
Lighting is provided both by modern wall fixtures and vintage stock.

Left
The space at the front of the shop has been left as double height for maximum impact.

The damaged upper floor was replaced with wood sourced from a local farm.

Right and below
The store, in Riga's
Bergs Bazaar, is named
after the building's
previous use.

Garage

RIGA, LATVIA
SIA ZAIGAS GAILES BIROJS
LAIME KAUGURE AND FRANCESKA KIRKE

Laima Kaugure is a Latvian designer with an international
profile. Her textiles appear at all the major trade fairs
around the world and she has collaborated with the likes
of Giorgio Armani Casa and Calvin Klein Home. Her idea, one
she had harboured for some time, was to open a store which
would champion the best of contemporary Latvian design.
'I have lived among, worked with, and spoken to all sorts
of people who all posed the same question: where in Riga,
or anywhere in Latvia, can one buy well-designed Latvian
gifts and products?' Hence, at the end of 2005 Kaugure,
together with renowned painter Franceska Kirke, opened
Garage, where the two take great care in sourcing the finest
handcrafted Latvian gifts. The shop is named after the
building's former use and is located in the capital's Bergs
Bazaar next to Hotel Bergs, a 'designer' operation housed in
a nineteenth-century building. Renovated in the early 1990s,
Bergs Bazaar is a chichi, cobbled quarter of specialist
boutiques, cafés, restaurants and galleries. This exclusive
pocket of tranquillity is a five-minute walk from Old Riga.
Garage showcases the latest work of popular local artists
and designers, whom Kaugure commissions. She describes
the products on show as 'exquisite and unusual items for
classical and extravagant people'.

Architectural work was carried out by SIA Zaigas Gailes Birojs, while the interior was designed by Kaugure and Kirke. And like many so-called lifestyle stores, Garage too has its refreshment area. 'After shopping on the ground floor, everyone is welcome to relax on a comfortable sofa on the upper floor – to taste coffee, cappuccino, tea with special biscuits, or fresh pressed juice,' states Kaugure.

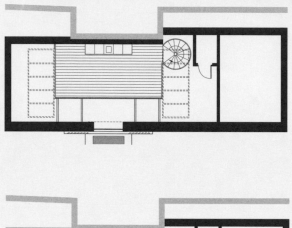

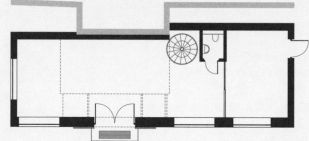

Above
The café is reached via
a spiral staircase.

Above right
From top: Mezzanine and
ground-floor plans.

Above
The mezzanine café area overlooks the retail space below.

Right
The glass-topped display case is lit by utilitarian pendant lights.

OBJECTS IN COMMON

Friend

SAN FRANSISCO, CALIFORNIA, USA
FUSEPROJECT

Friend by name and friendly by nature was the approach taken for the look of this San Francisco home décor store, which opened in 2003.

Fuseproject, also based in San Francisco, came up with an interiors scheme and branding which are intended to convey a warm, welcoming, personal style. So there are no 'cold, museum-like white walls', as Yves Béhar of fuseproject puts it, but instead 'a mixture of natural materials and fluid forms'. The reclaimed oak plank flooring was inspired by the city's weathered fishing docks. In other areas, there's a tartan material made of recycled tyres on the floor, 'providing a soft, resilient texture underfoot – a treat for shoppers who've been out pounding the pavement,' he says.

Throughout Friend, a series of 'nested' acrylic and oak display cases offers two opportunities for displaying merchandise: one on top of the acrylic surface, and the other underneath it on the oak surface. The oak planks are continued up the back wall, pausing only to allow a display space to showcase murals by different artists every three months. The store continues the recycled theme with its printed material and bags, which are made of recycled paper, 'reinforcing those same attributes at every touch with its customers,' says Béhar.

The display units have two levels: the oak 'table tops' and the acrylic casing that surrounds them.

There are also direct references to the shop's name. Béhar explains: 'Quotes about friendship are painted on other clear surfaces throughout the space, combining to make a warm, friendly and organic feel.' Meanwhile, Friend's logo and branding are drawn in a casual typeface to capture, says Béhar, the convivial mood of the shop. The lower case 'e' in the logotype tilts on its back, suggesting a smiling face – 'just the right image to evoke the warmth of being surrounded by friends'. Meanwhile, to add to the natural feel, hand-drawn blades of grass have been silk-screened onto the acrylic items.

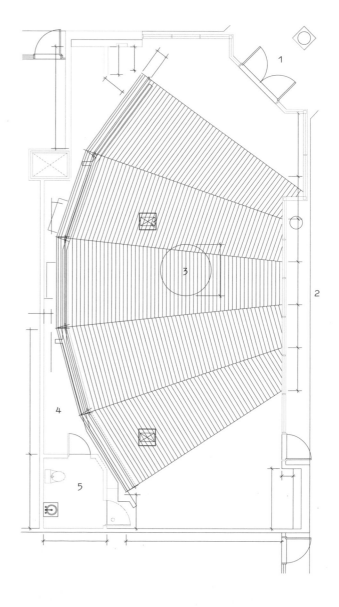

Above
The project's logo
features a 'smiling'
letter e.

Left
The 'e' is repeated as
a motif on the recycled
packaging.

Friend is the brainchild of Mark Lenox. Before Friend, he been a branding product development and marketing executive for a variety of companies including the Federated Department Stores and Birkenstock Footprint Sandals. 'In my travels around the world, I had become aware that there was a lot of great design that wasn't reaching the average customer [in San Francisco]. I felt that a store that catered to anyone interested in great design without all the "attitude" of many design stores would be welcome,' he explains.

Lenox stocks more than 50 names, from international players like Herman Miller, Kartell, Alessi and Vitra to local suppliers including Heath Ceramics, Pablo Lighting and Publique Living. He has located his venture in Hayes Valley, which he describes as a forgotten neighbourhood until 1989. 'Much of it was under a freeway overpass and the area had become quite run down. But after the San Francisco earthquake of 1989 brought down the overpass, the area embarked on a renaissance. Now, Hayes Valley is home to many unique and trendy boutiques, most independently owned and operated. It is visited by anyone looking for the latest in fashions and home décor.'

If Lenox has his way, this will not be his only Friend. 'I do feel that the concept is scalable to more stores.'

Above and right
The flooring of
reclaimed oak
planks curves up
to form the walls.

Artgadgets

EINDHOVEN, THE NETHERLANDS
MAURER UNITED ARCHITECTS

Artgadgets' customers should never get the feeling that they have entered one of those traditional 'chain stores'. This is the intention of Artgadgets' founder, Hans Theunissen. And to achieve this, any further outlets will stock locally sourced items, to sit alongside the existing international product range.

Artgadgets, whose home town is Eindhoven, was set up in 2004 as a magnet for trendy young things looking for the next exciting brand innovation. Theunissen describes these people as 'generation C', the 'C' standing for creative. As such, they are expected to be trendsetting, open-minded, art- and fashion- loving, and leaders in lifestyle and music.

The store's product range comprises what Theunissen describes as a varying assortment of wanna-haves, limited collections and must-haves – from sneakers, micro-electronic equipment and books and magazines on art, design and architecture, to actual fashion and haute couture. So the latest Adidas running shoes might rub shoulders with a brand of designer water.

As well pushing its retail business, Artgadgets also sees itself as a 'creative refuge where artists and creatives can meet, pollinate and entertain both themselves and their audience'. This all happens through events and product presentations.

All this is managed by a staff hand-picked to exude the appropriate brand values. The requirements are for them to be good-looking, service minded and experts in the latest developments in fashion, art, cults and music trends.

Theunissen is drawing on his experience in the art world in the creation of this format. For he is also the founder and director of Art Company, a consultancy and gallery which has advised listed multinationals on their acquisition of contemporary art. But he has a second hat, and as a graphic designer he has indulged his passion for design, trends and art.

Theunissen's debut outlet sits within the Piazza, a city centre shopping mall which has benefited from a revamp by architect Massimiliano Fuksas.

Maastricht-based Marc Maurer and Nicole Maurer of Maurer United Architects have given Artgadgets a pop-art inspired interior incorporating a glossy, red-and-white palette which contrasts with the industrial look of the gridded ceiling and fluorescent lighting.

The architects seem to have embraced the spirit of the store, and played with that in their choice of layout and materials. For example, as the mall is built of green glass, 'we did this shop in red glass, with just one green door to have a bit of fun,' explains Nicole.

Artgadgets' red and green sliding doors also hide a smaller door in the wall, so that with a pair of 3D glasses on you can see depth. 'It's a visual joke,' adds Marc Maurer. And of course, when the doors are positioned one on top of the other, they appear completely black.

Top left
The bright colour scheme contrasts with the tough industrial look of the gridded ceiling.

Bottom left
The main entrance is distinguished by its red glass windows.

This page
Stepped red seating with white cushions carry on the interior's red-and-white palette and offers patrons seating for performances and demonstrations.

Left
Objects are displayed as
if they were artworks in
a contemporary gallery.

Right
Customers are invited
to browse through books
for sale in the comfort
of the seating area

Below
Brilliant white floors
and walls are accented
by red and green acrylic
screens, and are an
apt backdrop for the
colourful art and
merchandise.

The red glass in the shopfront windows also means that
passers-by can't see the art from outside, so they have
to come in. And once inside, they're not distracted by
the shops outside.

Because of the complicated floorplan, the Maurers
created three overlapping walls to show art. 'That
meant we could put in a toilet for gallery visitors,
a little kitchen and some storage behind,' she adds.

The walls are also used to display art. But artists
don't have to rely on their own creativity. Each
neon light in the place is individually computer
controlled, to allow artists to create a lighting
composition or, indeed, a discotheque effect.

MUA put a shiny, white rubber on the floor to give extra
reflections. Meanwhile, the wide shelving, in white
plastic and lit with neon, is integrated with the wall
construction. The industrial-style ceiling has been
created by placing solid iron mesh below the existing
pipes and neon lights.

Right
The ceiling's bare tube lighting adds to the space's industrial, hi-tech feel.

Below
Detail of the red stepped seating area. Plastic cushions reflect the fluorescent lighting.

A specially designed piece of furniture acts as a meeting place, seating for presentations and a display area for art. Built over three levels, the reflecting fabric of its white cushions provides yet another light source.

A large and unexpected espresso machine has been given pride of place, positioned in such a way that one of Artgadgets' on-brand assistants must actually climb up the piece of furniture to make the coffee, turning even this simple act into a performance.

The store's pop-art-style font and logo are in keeping with the interior concept: 'We wanted it to be simple and contemporary. It's not a museum or a gallery, it's just a shop; it wants to be accessible,' Nicole explains.

Theunissen has earmarked a handful of trendy cities for his next stops, including Antwerp, Barcelona, Berlin, Milan, Paris and London. Meanwhile in The Netherlands, he has his eye on Amsterdam and Rotterdam.

CHAPTER 3
FASHION
AND
ACCESSORIES

'Fashion has the most potential for small independent stores. Consumers are more demanding of fashion retailers,' says Richard Perks of the retail research company Mintel. And, indeed, there are enough good-looking fashion one-offs around the world for a separate book. These places are often competing with the fashion label chains or department stores, so retail design is vital to pull in shoppers off the street.

You can't get much more stunning than Thanks in Mumbai. Its owner sees it as up against the 'monobrand' stores Louis Vuitton, Dior, Bvlgari and Salvatore Ferragamo. But this amazing black, moulded affair bears little resemblance to the gallery-style white boxes of many high-end international brands. According to Chris Lee, one of Thanks's designers, this is intentional: 'Retail design itself is typically following Western trends and models, with "mainstream minimal" as the contemporary aesthetic.' Guy Zucker, designer of Delicatessen in Tel Aviv, calls this 'the big bore of bourgeois minimalism', which he sees in his home town of New York's Madison Avenue. He suggests that it is in the Lower East Side or TriBeCa that 'suddenly you bump into something more experimental and rough'.

Purple Shop in Helsinki is also up against the multichain giants. This accessory store has competition on all sides from Swedish Glitter, British Accessorize and Finnish Ninja. Its look, though, should help it stand out as it is a cheap and cheerful take on the great outdoors, complete with plastic trees.

Delicatessen uses a strong design concept, as well, to make a big noise on a small budget. This is a single brand shop for a fashion designer where the concept is all about low cost materials making a statement about the very product – fashion – on display. Other places stray towards the lifestyle sector, either by stocking a few items beyond clothes and accessories, or, like Bangalore's Grasshopper, by offering refreshment too. Of course, such cross-pollination is also happening in the chain world, with Zara, for example, introducing a line of home ware.

THANKS

MUMBAI, INDIA
CHRIS LEE AND KAPIL GUPTA

Ashish Chordia plotted his attack on the nascent Indian luxury market while he was working in management consultancy. He saw the potential for luxury in his homeland and started planning the creation of what he calls India's first luxury retail brand, naming it Thanks.

Once Chordia had secured exclusivity rights from the European luxury houses, he then needed an appropriate environment to accommodate them. The store, which opened in 2005, is seemingly well positioned in the south Mumbai neighbourhood of Worli. 'This area is becoming the focus with major multinational companies locating their offices there, and one of India's biggest malls, Atria, opening. The street now offers an interesting mix of restaurants, retail and entertainment,' he claims. Chordia is out to attract a high-end, internationally minded crowd comprising the newly affluent generation of CEOs and other senior professionals in their thirties and early forties, entrepreneurs and returning 'prodigal children'. Brands stocked include Dolce e Gabbana, Prada, Fendi, Sergio Rossi, Juicy Couture, Marc Jacobs and Pucci.

Right
Thanks's interior was
required to compete with
international luxury
retailers and appeal to
India's growing elite.

88

Left
The extraordinary
double-curved ribbon was
an artisanal as much as
a technological feat.

Right
The curved three-
dimensional forms were
built by craftsmen using
traditional methods.
The MDF cladding was
then painted in high-
gloss automotive paint.

Below
Plan
1 Entry
2 Shop 2
3 Stair to mezzanine
4 Cash counter
5 Shop 4
6 Shop 5
7 Multibrand area
8 Shop 6
9 Shop 3
10 Entry to multibrand
   area
11 Shop 1
12 Staff room
13 Guest toilet

Chris Lee and Kapil Gupta have practices in London and
Mumbai respectively, but also collaborate. They were
given the brief to create a suitably eye-catching retail
environment. This store had to compete not with other
multibrand outlets, but with international monobrand
stores such as Louis Vuitton, Dior, Bvlgari and Salvatore
Ferragamo. So it was up to Gupta and Lee to create a
unifying aesthetic and design experience that would not
only define Thanks as a new fashion house but evolve the
usual shop-in-shop approach of department stores into
a cohesive whole.

Chordia's 700 square metre (7,535 square foot) space was
set within a diagonal column grid and had an existing
mezzanine that lowered the ceiling over the multibrand
area to a potentially claustrophobic 2.4 metres (8 feet).
The two architects resolved this problem by placing
a café and lounge bar on this level. 'The design seeks
to organize and regulate the shopping experience into
a sequence of focus and attention points,' explains Lee.
The effect is created with bent ceilings, graduated floor
shades, skewed pedestals and twisted columns. 'The fluid
geometry of the interior and a glowing PVC ceiling induce
movement, drawing the shopper into the belly of the
store,' Gupta adds.

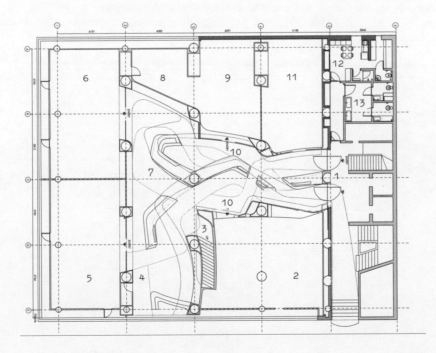

The merchandising and display systems have been carved into the double-curved surfaces of the store. Meanwhile, black and white automotive paint, Corian-clad furniture, faux leather and rubber floors were specified to emphasize 'a monochromatic, synthetic and seamless formal order, a seductive backdrop for a luxury shopping experience', says Lee. The whole is one shiny, liquid ribbon, a blending of display systems, partitions, seats, counters and ceiling. 'We created a continuous monolithic object that pushed the boundaries of construction in India,' Gupta adds.

The original idea for the three-dimensional geometries was to make them in fibreglass through a local automotive body-part manufacturer, who seemed to have the skills to sculpt double-curved and ruled surfaces. However, the duo soon realized that local carpenters could hand-carve extremely complex parts out of mere MDF. Lee and Gupta explain that their tricky three-dimensional drawings, designed using CAD software, were hand-traced onto blocks of fibreboard, before being hand-sculpted into the desired form. 'The precision achieved by these craftsmen using almost primitive working tools was astonishing,' they say. No little saving was made by ditching the fibreglass, and the MDF surface was then painted with automotive paint to achieve a high-gloss finish. The architects put the success of the project down to this marrying of cutting-edge software and low-tech construction methods with local craft traditions.

Left and below
Lighting can be changed in the mezzanine café and lounge to alter the mood.

ACRYLIC

TOKYO, JAPAN
KLEINDYTHAM ARCHITECTURE AND MASAKO BAN

'Pet architecture' is the rather cuddly term for structures built in the awkward little sites that are left between big, new developments in Tokyo. But as awkward as they are, they have also given architects something to get their teeth into. Tokyo-based Yasuhiro Yamashita's polygonal but bijou Mineral House is a case in point. KleinDytham architecture was asked to turn one such site into a retail opportunity by property investment company RISA Partners. The space is located in the swanky international area of Minato, which is peppered with embassies and expats, about one kilometre (0.6 miles) from the large Roppongi Hills development. This was the architects' smallest project to date – an 11 metre (36 foot) long, two-storey high wedge, 2.5 metres (8 feet) wide at one end and tapering to just 600 millimetres (24 inches) at the other. And in order to attract a retailer to such a bijou spot, RISA took the unusual step of allowing the architects to design it before a tenant had even been found. 'We said to the developers, build an unusual building and it will act as a large ad,' says Mark Dytham.

Above left to right
The narrow site is all façade, allowing the architects to play with the appearance of the glass to attract attention day and night.

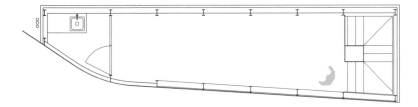

Top left and right
The bamboo motif
on the glass creates
a pleasing shadow
effect on Acrylic's
jewellery and
accessories.

Above
The plan shows just
how narrow the space
really is.

The unit's shape means it's dominated by its façade. So KDa
set about decorating it with a graphic image of a bamboo
grove stencilled in white on the glass. Meanwhile, inside,
the back wall was painted bright green. 'By day, the graphic
becomes a striking and simple form of sun-shading; by
night, green light dapples over the road – a luminous bamboo
plantation in the heart of the metropolis,' says Dytham.
All the effort paid off, as the unit quickly attracted
Masako Ban, the wife of Japanese architect Shigeru Ban, who
was looking to open her first shop for Acrylic, her playful,
geometric jewellery brand. In 2005 she moved in: 'I feel
like I'm basking in the woods with my favourite green,' she
says of the interiors. As luck would have it, the green
of the wall is the same colour as Acrylic's brand identity.

Ban, whose designs are stocked in Osaka, New York, London
and Copenhagen, says the store is bringing in a creative
clientele, from artists to architects. Her minimal
interiors, with their simple furniture, work well against
the shadows of the window illustration. The wall pegs
accommodate the bag range she produces with her sister,
Tomoko Nakamura. The effect is more art gallery than shop.
If the space hadn't attracted a tenant, KDa would have
peeled away the bamboo graphic, replacing it with another
eye-catching idea.

NICHOLAS JAMES

LONDON, UK, GIDDINGS DESIGN

The street of Hatton Garden on the edge of the City of London is synonymous with jewellery and the diamond trade. Nearly every shop is a family-owned jewellers or wholesaler where, traditionally, betrothed couples come to hunt down the perfect sparkler.

But while retail experiences and consumer tastes have moved on, Hatton Garden has not. Most of the outlets look as if they haven't changed for the last few generations. Chandeliers, carpets and dark wood panelling abound, as do little silky cushions on which the jewellery is laid in the window, in front of a curtain blocking the view into the store. However, this old-school approach to retail looks as if it is gradually dying out. 'There is a move towards smartening up,' says Nick Fitch.

In fact, Fitch himself is a pioneer of the movement to smarten up. His store, Nicholas James, is a temple to modern design, and would not look out of place on London's Bond Street. As such, it is likely to alienate many old-school Hatton Gardeners, but that's not something that seems to bother him.

Above
The vast glass façade stands out in Hatton Garden.

Right
The large interior space is light, bright and unashamedly modern.

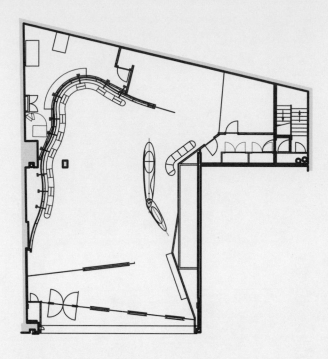

Fitch joined his father's diamond trading business in 1986. He started to produce commissioned jewellery and realized that this was his bent. He had always harboured desires to have his own shop and he opened his first store ('quirky, eclectic and off the beaten track') just off Hatton Garden in 1992. He took the plunge and moved Nicholas James to the Garden proper in 2005, confident that there was a gap in the market. 'Having worked there all my life, I had proof of a type of customer looking for something a bit different.'

Like Fitch, Giddings Design, his retail design agency, had a history of working in the jewellery industry with clients including Cartier and De Beers. 'I have been in the business for 20 years, and I've become so dissatisfied with the state of most English jewellers,' says Mark Giddings. 'We were getting so far behind the rest of the world.' He describes the brief for Nicholas James as the shortest he's ever received: 'Nick said, "I want 95 per cent of people walking up Hatton Garden to go 'yuk' and five per cent to say 'that's where I want to spend my money'. Push the boundaries".'

The result is a slightly space-age interior with lots of white, clever LED lighting and minimal product on show. 'I wanted it to be very spacious. Most jewellers aren't. I wanted it to be modern, slightly futuristic. At one point, I said Kubrick's 2001,' says Fitch, describing the interior as being almost clinical, but in a good way. 'It's a big space and it needed to be structured with layers,' says Giddings. Hence the angled glass wall at the front and the funnel effect so that people don't have to walk straight into this large, potentially intimidating interior. Fitch was so concerned with this aspect that a 3D CAD walk-through was mocked up before construction work went ahead.

To add to the welcoming effect, the left-hand wall is scalloped with curvy panelling, and in the middle of the store stands a folly of sorts. This structure, created by Giddings, comprises three elliptical display units on pedestals. The thick glass of the showcases swivels open. 'We wanted to create another area of display that was sculptural and acted as a point of interest,' says Fitch.

Far left
A glass corridor gives customers a less threatening route into the large and spacious shop.

Left
Plan. The entrance and glass façade are at the bottom.

Right
At the back of the shop, there is a seating area for consultations.

Below
The elliptical display cases add another point of interest to the spacious showroom.

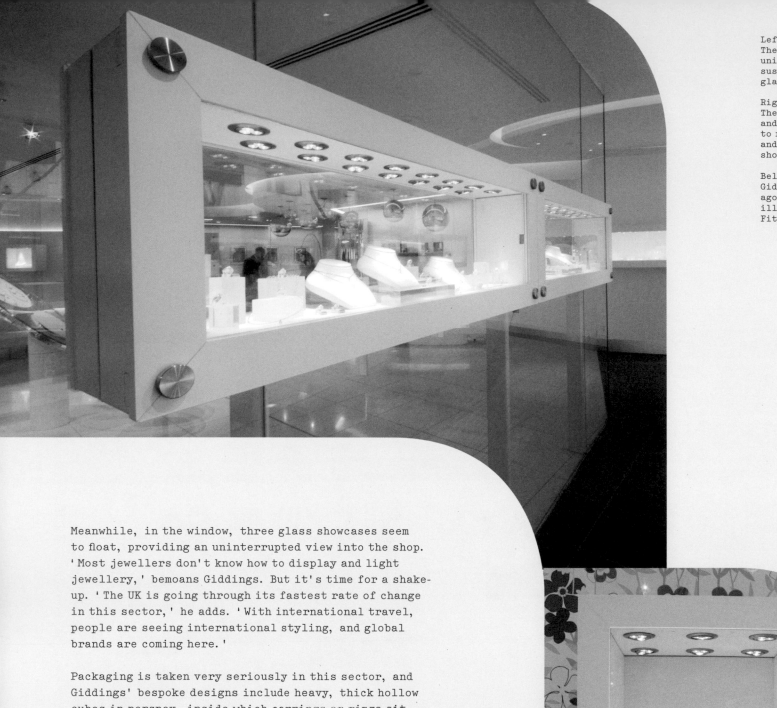

Left
The window display
units appear to be
suspended in the
glass.

Right
The bespoke packaging
and boxes are intended
to reflect the style
and quality of the
shop's environment.

Below
Giddings Design
agonized over the
illumination of
Fitch's creations.

Meanwhile, in the window, three glass showcases seem
to float, providing an uninterrupted view into the shop.
'Most jewellers don't know how to display and light
jewellery,' bemoans Giddings. But it's time for a shake-
up. 'The UK is going through its fastest rate of change
in this sector,' he adds. 'With international travel,
people are seeing international styling, and global
brands are coming here.'

Packaging is taken very seriously in this sector, and
Giddings' bespoke designs include heavy, thick hollow
cubes in perspex, inside which earrings or rings sit
on a magnetic box. There's also a coloured bag within
a transparent bag, aiming to reflect the lightness of the
shop itself.

Fitch likes the idea of opening further Nicholas
Jameses, perhaps in New York rather than in the UK. But,
realistically, he admits, 'I would rather do one really
well than build a little empire. I don't have global
empire aspirations.'

PLATFORM SOUL

HOBOKEN, NEW JERSEY, USA
KEANE + TIMM

More of a gallery for shoes than a conventional-looking shoe shop, this tiny space is the brainchild of a fashion alumna of Rhode Island School of Design.

Desire Peters opened Platform Soul in 2005 'because the public only gets exposure to the high-quality shoes in the large fashion houses… Some of these places only hold collections for a short time, and it's hard to find a theme under one roof.' Her stock includes the big names such as Marni, Prada, Gucci, Manolo Blahnik and Jimmy Choo.

Keane + Timm's design is intended to allow the 900 square metre (9,688 square foot) interior to change its look around Peters' changing themes. 'The store changes in appearance quite a bit due to stock and colouration of the materials, lights and such like,' explains Patrick Keane of Keane + Timm, which was also responsible for the graphics. The idea is that passers-by will be lured in by the frequent changes. Peters says that the design works really well 'with the seasons and the themes that we work with'.

Above
The look of Platform Soul
sits comfortably in this
Hoboken street.

Top right
More gallery than
conventional retail
space, Keane + Timm's
design is pleasingly
sparse.

Bottom right
Colourful shoeboxes
double as décor behind
heavy-duty glass walls.

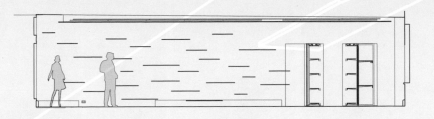

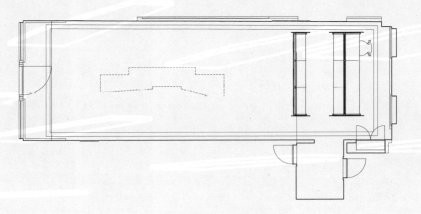

Keane + Timm has manufactured this flexibility through the
display systems. 'The shelves on the walls can be interchanged
infinitely and randomly - depending on how many shoes the owner
wants to display - by an invisible system of pins,' Keane explains.
'The blade-like dichronic glass comes in a host of colours,
and it can be adapted to suit seasons or ranges, so autumn might
be a host of browns and greens, for example. The lighting too
can be adjusted to different hues.' These shelves also add
to the gallery feel. 'Rather than the shoes being displayed
traditionally, they are placed on the wall as a series of
art objects, as the owner likes to have openings with every
collection,' Keane adds. Even the shoeboxes are made to
contribute. They are as colourful and varied as the shoes
themselves. 'They're on display in the back, behind some heavy-
duty structural glass shelving systems, since they are also
very attractive,' says Keane, 'and they add to the colour and
texture of the store.'

As for Platform Soul's size, Peters claims that 'people like
the intimacy of the store'. And while she admits that this one
outlet is very hard work, 'give us another year, and we will
do something on (Manhattan's) Bleecker Street'.

Delicatessen is an example of the concept store
taken to its extreme. The brain behind the design
is New York-based Guy Zucker, and like many a
designer in this sort of situation, what was lacking
in fees was made up for in imagination.

Zucker was tasked with creating a store for a
fashion label. Idit Barak, who had studied fashion
in New York, returned home to Tel Aviv to open her
boutique as she saw many of the bigger fashion
brands there but few smaller offers. 'It's a
concept store,' she says of Delicatessen. 'It's
not pretty.' This immediately distances it from
many Israeli retail spaces, which she describes
as beautiful but not conceptual. The fact that
Delicatessen, which opened in 2005, is so eye-
catching has paid off in terms of acknowledgement
from the media both at home and abroad.

DELICATESSEN

TEL AVIV, ISREAL, Z-A/GUY ZUCKER

Right
Zucker turns
cardboard tubes into
a sculpture- cum-
merchandising unit.

Below
The tools of designer
Barak's trade are
strategically
positioned in the
window alongside the
finished product.

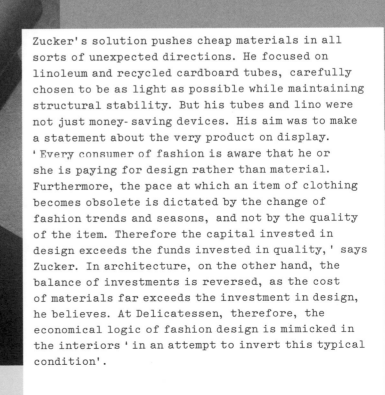

Zucker's solution pushes cheap materials in all
sorts of unexpected directions. He focused on
linoleum and recycled cardboard tubes, carefully
chosen to be as light as possible while maintaining
structural stability. But his tubes and lino were
not just money- saving devices. His aim was to make
a statement about the very product on display.
'Every consumer of fashion is aware that he or
she is paying for design rather than material.
Furthermore, the pace at which an item of clothing
becomes obsolete is dictated by the change of
fashion trends and seasons, and not by the quality
of the item. Therefore the capital invested in
design exceeds the funds invested in quality,' says
Zucker. In architecture, on the other hand, the
balance of investments is reversed, as the cost
of materials far exceeds the investment in design,
he believes. At Delicatessen, therefore, the
economical logic of fashion design is mimicked in
the interiors ' in an attempt to invert this typical
condition'.

107

Zucker's choice of materials had a strong impact on the actual layout of the store and dictated the forms and functional possibilities. 'The display elements were shaped following the structural abilities of the cardboard tubes, and the display fins use the flexible qualities of the linoleum,' says Zucker, who happily took advantage of both the grey and yellow sides of the lino.

Barak points out that when big chain stores open an outlet, they have researchers telling them the laws of retail. 'Because it's a small collection, I didn't need a lot of display space, so we could make a display that was less practical. We didn't even think of income per square foot.' And by keeping the interiors cheap, Barak will feel able to change the whole lot in a couple of years, if she likes. She's already considering more outlets, but has no wish to set up an Israel-only chain. 'More and more local fashion designers are starting to sell outside Israel,' she says.

Below
Mobile screens give
Barak spatial options
in the small store.

108

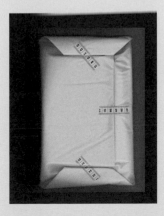

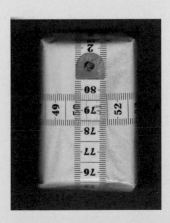

Above
Model seen from above.
A ribbon of grey
extends round the
walls, uniting the
space.

Left
The tailoring theme
is continued on the
packaging.

CHAN LUU

LOS ANGELES, CALIFORNIA, USA
MARMOL RADZINER + ASSOCIATES

Chan Luu arrived in the US from Vietnam in 1972. Three years later she had a degree in fashion design from the Fashion Institute of Design and Merchandising Los Angeles.

As a jewellery and fashion designer, Luu has a string of corporate showrooms in downtown Los Angeles, New York, Dallas and Atlanta. Her products are stocked across the globe in such salubrious environments as Neiman Marcus, Saks Fifth Avenue and Bergdorf Goodman in the US; Harvey Nichols in London; and Isetan and Mitsukoshi in Japan.

What's more, her pieces turn up in the glossy magazines including Vogue, Elle, Glamour, Harper's Bazaar and InStyle. She also has a celebrity following in the shape of Jennifer Aniston, Mischa Barton, Sandra Bullock, Christina Aguilera, Britney Spears, Drew Barrymore and Janet Jackson.

Despite all this exposure and coverage, in 2002 Luu felt that she needed her own retail space for her clothes and accessories, as well as her jewellery. 'My flagship store is showcasing my complete collection, where editorial people and buyers can come and view my whole concept and vision.'

The 111 square metre (1,200 square foot) boutique is on Robertson Boulevard, which Luu describes as 'the hottest street in LA', and its positioning makes it easier for her to service people from the movie industry.

Luu wanted the space not only to showcase her work, but also to encourage punters to linger. Los Angeles-based Marmol Radziner executed this brief with particular focus on tactile surfaces. 'We've created a warm composition of sand-blasted birch plank complemented with cool stainless steel,' explains Leo Marmol.

Left
For a tactile effect,
sand-blasted birch
plank rubs shoulders
with stainless steel.

Right
Vintage light fixtures
are complemented by
recessed halogen
spotlights.

Below right
The cases,
furnishings and wall
panelling were all
custom-made for the
shop.

He and Ron Radziner fabricated custom-designed casework,
furnishings and wall panelling from the same understated
materials. Meanwhile, modular display cases with glass-
covered drawers, balanced by stainless-steel shelving
along birch walls, are intended to 'further enhance the
intimate space' according to Radziner.

It was imperative to Luu that her customers be able
to actually interact with her merchandise. 'To that
end, the display cases and shelves were designed to
provide easy access,' says Marmol. 'When moving through
the interior, visitors experience a reflective play of
light and surface as the gems' brilliant hues sparkle
against the raw wood surfaces and steel details. Vintage
industrial pendant light fixtures and recessed halogens
create a warm glow throughout the store.'

Luu has no intention of opening any further outlets.
'We are really focusing on wholesale business,' she says.

GUYS & DOLLS

Only those with fashion retail in their blood might feel confident enough to open a shop without carrying out any market research. This is what sisters Sarah and Sabrina Ettedgui did, their uncle being Joseph Ettedgui, founder of Joseph, which their father Franklin helped set up. 'Sarah was doing Montessori training,' explains Sabrina. 'I became pregnant after university and was not employable but needed a job. Within a week we had the idea and the site.'

Their idea was a high-end children's clothes shop, and the site was on Walton Street, a road of many independent boutiques and which well-heeled shoppers walk down on their way to Harrods. The sisters were recommended the London designers Sybarite by their uncle. 'When constructing and fitting out the new Marni store on London's Sloane Street, Sybarite built a good relationship with Joseph Ettedgui, with whom Marni was swapping store locations,' says Simon Mitchell at Sybarite, a breakaway group from Future Systems. Sybarite then found themselves working for Joseph, and when a children's shop was mooted, their name was suggested to the sisters.

Despite the lack of market research, Sarah and Sabrina had clear notions about what they required. 'We wanted it to be a children's shop,' says Sabrina, which means a shop designed with children in mind. 'Mothers weren't shopping with their children; instead they would buy something and bring it back if it was the wrong size or they didn't like it.' This seemed like madness to Guys & Dolls' owners and Sybarite has made the environment so child friendly that children and their mothers or carers can happily spend an hour in the store. 'We decided in the early planning stages that the most effective way to approach the brief was to put ourselves in a child's shoes, most importantly considering their height and perspective on the world, including colour and shapes,' says Mitchell.

The bespoke
spiralling rail and
the round display
units echo the
circular motif of the
branding.

The result is a low-rise, primary-coloured play area bedecked in designer gear. Along with a ball pod at the front of the store, there are toys and crayons available for the customers' enjoyment. And, what's more, there are no sharp edges – the floor is grey rubber and the walls are gently banked, making them pleasing slides. Leading on from Sybarite's circle-inspired logo, much of the interior is similarly shaped, from the round, diminutive changing rooms to the door handles, drawers and the spiral rail hanger that runs all along one side of the shop. 'Everything is bespoke – we were particularly pleased with the rail as it fits the concept perfectly and is an excellent solution to maximizing merchandise in a small space,' Mitchell adds. The sisters seem to be suitably impressed by Sybarite's solution: 'We didn't envisage anything like this. It is like a concept store,' says Sabrina.

Now they have settled in Walton Street, the Ettedguis realize there is local competition, but none of it direct. On the same road there is Marie-Chantal and Caramel, which Sabrina describes respectively as classic and neutral.

And while it's early days for Guys & Dolls, Sabrina admits that Sarah and she have had ideas for expansion since they opened: 'We don't want to expand too quickly. But we would like to open for teenagers because there is a gap in the market.'

Above left
The colourful circular theme is carried on into the store's branding.

Above right
The rounded shape and low level of the display units make them especially child friendly.

THE CORNER BERLIN

BERLIN, GERMANY
JOSEF VOELK AND EMMANUEL DE BAYSER

The Corner Berlin is born out of two people's experiences in the luxury industry. Josef Voelk started his career in luxury in the US, as managing director of Bottega Veneta, and then as managing director of Giorgio Armani's west coast operations, followed by Armani in Germany. Before setting up The Corner Berlin, Emmanuel de Bayser was international communications director of Giorgio Armani perfumes and fragrances at L'Oreal.

The impetus to open The Corner was a desire ' to start our own adventure, pulling together all the things we like and putting them together in one space,' explains de Bayser. The spot they chose is opposite the Französische Dom on what they call the city's most beautiful square, the Gendarmenmarkt. This area is becoming the glamorous international-chic area of Berlin, with Rocco Forte opening a luxury hotel next door.

Since opening in 2006, The Corner's stock has been dominated by unashamedly high-end clothing, from Alaia, Balenciaga, Marc Jacobs, Givenchy, Stella McCartney and Alexander McQueen to Burberry Prorsum, Balmain, Derek Lam and Rick Owens. There are also lifestyle pieces thrown in, in the shape of carefully chosen beauty products, electronics, books, music, film, art and twentieth-century vintage design and furniture. And like many such fashion-cum-lifestyle destinations, customers can continue to live the brand by nipping into the café for refreshments. The Corner is consequently attracting bourgeois west Berliners, and avant-garde east Berliners, as well as other Germans and internationals.

With its 18 windows, the three-floored store is very light. 'We wanted to create an open, simple, modern space with complete transparency on to the breathtaking historical square,' says de Bayser, who created the space with Voelk. Colour plays an

Left and below
Vintage furniture is
on display, but fashion
dominates.

important role in the design. 'Our colour range runs from a very dark brown, almost black, at the store's entrance, to off-white at the rear,' explains de Bayser, 'with intermediary colours being khaki, grey and beige tones.' These are all painted in a lacquer finish, to add light to the space. The basement's walls are graded from dark brown to beige, and grey to white, which helps with the layout of the different rooms of men's and women's fashion. The art collection is also down there. Merchandising units come in the form of simple portable cubes of different sizes that can all be combined. 'This gives us endless display options all around the store,' says de Bayser, who changes the merchandising concept every two weeks. Much of the lifestyle pieces, as well as the restaurant, are on the ground floor, with accessories and denim on the mezzanine.

The clever use of paving stones inside suggests the continuation of the pavement outside. The merchandising units are a pale shiny grey to complement the stone floor, and to allow the merchandise to stand out.

For Berlin, this concept is unique, claims de Bayser: 'There is still in Berlin a lot to do in terms of style. The art scene is at a top international level, but we are not yet there in terms of style.' In fact, it's de Bayser's belief that Germany, on the whole, is lacking when it comes to high style. 'Apart from mono label brands which have standard international high-end stores, luxury retail in Germany still lacks an international individual vision; there's still a lot of room to experiment in this field.'

It's true that Berlin has a sort of unassuming boho grunginess which would seem to eschew too much overt gentrification, and one of the reasons why de Bayser and Voelk chose Berlin was that 'all the other capitals in Europe or in developed parts of the world are already saturated'. Despite that, the owners do like the idea of setting up Corners in other European cities.

Right
The mezzanine houses
the shop's denim
collection.

Below left
The pale grey
merchandising units
complement the stone
floor at the entrance.

Below right
The store is opposite
Französische Dom on
Berlin's Gendarmenmarkt.

Left
The imposing arched
doorways on the ground
floor are 4 metres (13
feet) high and 1 metre
(3 feet 3 inches) deep.
Each frame is lined with
black painted steel.

Right
Sleek sliding clothes
rails contrast with the
ornate light fittings
on the first floor.

2006FEB01

VIENNA, AUSTRIA, BEHF

This independent fashion store is up against
some serious competition as Prada, Gucci, Bally,
Cartier, Louis Vuitton, Chanel, Hermes and
Versace are all in the neighbourhood. 2006Feb01
is located down a narrow street in the historic
centre of Vienna, in the main shopping district
on Plankengasse 3. The site backs onto a tranquil
garden in the Kapuzinergruft courtyard, an
attribute of which Viennese architects BEHF took
advantage in their scheme. 'The shop was designed
to be unique in its cozy, private atmosphere,
a place to relax in and which expressed the
Viennese identity of its two owners,' explains

Stephan Ferenczy, BEHF's managing director.
The owners, Horst Payrhuber and Manfred
Staudacher, are seasoned fashion retailers,
having previously owned and run Vienna's Helmut
Lang boutique.

They've stocked their own venture with
established international men's and women's
designers, including Viktor & Rolf, Aquascutum,
Alexander McQueen and Loewe.

In BEHF's design, the shop opens both onto the street in front and the garden behind. 'The garden and the street are "floating" in the shop,' says Ferenczy, 'so inside there is a "street" area and a "garden" area.' That means the vast façade is designed to suit both the historic stone front and the modern interior. The architects have installed 4 metre (13 foot) high dark glass elements which offer broken views to the interior from the street. Central, private shopping zones on the ground and first floors are cordoned off with pale drapes. This is a neat and tidy environment in purple and cream, with a sense of grandeur that's in keeping with the stock. To the rear the garden is echoed by a bold floral wallpaper on the walls and ceilings of the changing rooms.

As for the name, 'We wanted to have something different, not a name like Boutique Gigi, Colette, or some such. We wanted to have something like a code,' explains Staudacher, so they chose the shop's opening date. He and Payrhuber have no intention of following this with other outlets, whatever the date.

Left
Pale drapes separate the two private shopping areas from the rest of the boutique.

Below left
From top: first- and ground-floor plans.

Below
The ornate, vegetal patterned wallpaper in the changing room alludes to the courtyard garden behind the store.

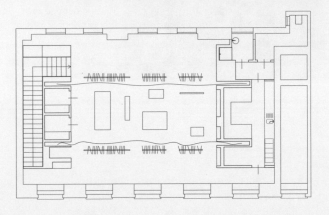

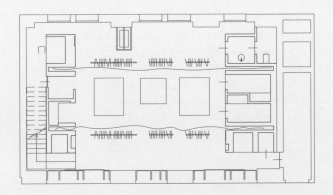

GRASSHOPPER

BANGALORE, INDIA
DYAN BELLIAPPA

'We had been making clothes for so many years and already had a clientele; and there's not much going on in Bangalore' - two good reasons for Himanshu Dimri and Sonali Sattar to open Grasshopper. But rather than setting up shop in Bangalore proper, they entice their followers to a farm 40 minutes from the city centre. This is the family property where the couple built a new structure to house their enterprise on a site that had previously been paddy fields.

Dimri and Sattar, both graduates of New Delhi's National Institute of Fashion Technology, launched their label Hidden Harmony in 1993. They trusted their emporium's design to local architect Dyan Belliappa and it opened in 2002. He was tasked with creating something that would work within the vernacular - many of the surrounding farm buildings are in local grey stone masonry - and could accommodate designer clothing along with an exhibition space and restaurant.

Grasshopper's owners wanted it to be one big volume, so Belliappa came up with a concept that looks like a contemporary take on the urban warehouse. 'In our initial discussions there was also some talk about having part of the building below ground,' explains Belliappa, 'but the high level of subsoil water ruled this out because of the cost implications.'The proposed site turned out to have a slight depression at one end, which allowed the architect to configure the approach straight into an upper mezzanine. The entrance at this level looks onto a single, vast area broken up by lights and display forms hanging at different levels. The upstairs gallery leads to a staircase that takes you to the shop below which then flows outdoors to the restaurant.

Left
The architect worked within the local stone.

Below
The alfresco restaurant is run by one of the owners.

The store's design is intended to blend two metaphors: the traditional Indian market or street, and the fashion ramp. 'And from a design perspective, the space needed to be able to handle retail – an activity associated with urbanity – in a setting which could be described as semirural (though urbanization has now caught up with a vengeance),' Belliappa says. 'As garments and accessories were at the core of the store, the background needed to be a neutral colour,' he adds. To complement the surrounding farm buildings he picked grey and used concrete in its various forms, right down to the polished floor. Exposed concrete in corrugated and rough textures adds contrast to the finely crafted clothing and products within.

As well as Hidden Harmony, other designers featured include A Small Shop by Anshu Arora Sen, Free Falling by Aparna Jagdhari, Ice Silver by Anu Nagarkatte, Libelulle by Joe Ikareth, Gaurav Gupta, Puja Nayyar, Savio Jon and Sujit Mukherjee. 'We introduced new designers because we felt it would make the space more interesting, and because we also felt that Bangalore lacked the kind of products we would be retailing, and therefore was in need of a specialized store,' Sattar explains. She also ensures that what she stocks is not available elsewhere in the city.

All Grasshopper's graphics are the work of Ninan Joseph, and Sattar is particularly pleased with their brightly coloured, reversible fabric bags.

Given that Sattar and Dimri are so personally involved (Dimri runs the restaurant), no further Grasshoppers are planned.

Above
Corrugated and unfinished textures contrast with the attention to detail in the clothing.

Above right
Concrete is used in many forms, including for the polished floor.

Left
The subdued colour
palette of the
concrete and stone
provides a neutral
foil for the bright
clothing.

Below
Visitors enter via the
mezzanine level, with
a view of the shop floor
spread out below them.

PURPLE SHOP

HELSINKI, FINLAND, M41LH2

'We wanted to reflect the sort of bric-a-brac feeling of the goods in the interior design, and make the best of a very tight budget,' says M41LH2 designer Johanna Hyrkäs. Her solution for this accessories shop, which opened in 2006, was a kitsch take on the Finnish landscape. The floor is covered with standard 'plastic grass' in metallic green, and the wall graphic – created by Hyrkäs – features pictures of mountains and pines. 'These images act as a strong, space-creating element as well as a backdrop for hanging bags and such like,' she explains. Meanwhile, smaller goods are displayed on little plastic trees, the same colour as the floor. The sales counter also reflects the budget – it's an old cupboard found through a Web auction. But only by glancing up could Purple's customers take in Hyrkäs' most innovative element: 100 millimetre (4 inch) wide plastic strips are strung below ugly fluorescent lamps. 'This was a low-budget solution and makes the ceiling look a little bit like clouds and also allowed the sprinkler, HVAC and existing light installations to remain as they were,' she says.

Purple Shop was set up by Petri Koivurinne, a year after he graduated from the Helsinki School of Economics. 'I wanted to start my own business, and at the time there weren't really any fashion accessories stores in Helsinki.' Since then, a handful of multinationals have turned up, but as the accessories sector is growing in Finland, Koivurinne is confident that there is room for everyone. He opened in Forum, the city's busiest mall. 'This shopping centre is probably the most popular place for young people to do fashion shopping,' he says. However, it's not just his original target market of 15- to 29-year-old women who frequent Purple Shop. 'Now I've seen that many of my customers are between 30 and 50.'

Perhaps, in style terms, the shop would be as comfortable out of the mall and in the streets of Uudenmaankatu and Fredrikinkatu in the city centre, where Hyrkäs observes the most interesting stores can be found. In fact, Koivurinne has since closed this shop and reopened on Ateneuminkuja, a small street full of boutiques.

Above left
A kitsch take on Finland's
great outdoors complete
with plastic fir trees.

Above right
Plastic sheeting across
the ceiling hides the air
conditioning and doubles
as stylized clouds.

Right
The shop's logo (seen here
on a bag) was designed by
Kalle Palmunen.

Chapter 4
Random
Gems

While food, home ware and fashion are the most popular categories for one-off retailers, there are pockets of activity elsewhere. Cosmetics is a popular sector, as consumers' tastes increasingly vie away from the mass-produced unctions and unguents served up by most shopping street chemists and department stores towards more niche brands. The popular cosmetics brands Sephora and Space.NK. must surely have inspired others with their success. The upshot is newcomers such as Breathe in Berlin, created by Roomsafari. But cosmetics and skincare have evolved in recent times into well-being, which has been carved up further still by the opening of a few outlets aimed specifically at men. JHP-designed Wholeman in London and Spruce in Brighton by Platform have arrived to do battle with a couple of established players, including The Refinery. And in Paris, Emmanuel Fenasse's interiors for Skeen are finding favour with female customers as well as the target male shoppers.

Despite the strength of global and national book chains, and increasing competition from the Internet everywhere, as well as supermarkets in some countries, budding book shop owners will not be put off.

One such couple, who have realized their dream and created the interiors to boot are Kenny Leck and Karen Wai of Singapore's BooksActually. And there are examples of small and interesting stores which now boast a handful of outlets, such as Decitre, a seven-strong bookshop chain in the Alps. Meanwhile, Kid's Republic is a niche book shop, in that it stocks only children's books. The Beijing outlet, designed by SKSK Architects also in Beijing, is for the Japanese publisher Poplar, so not strictly owned by entrepreneurs. Still,

it's a great-looking space with its colourful ribbons 'wrapping' the space, and is getting much attention in a country unaccustomed to speciality book shops.

Other forms of entertainment also interest entrepreneurs, such as music, in the form of Pause Ljud & Bild entertainment store in Stockholm by Bas Brand.

Then there are the genuine innovators, which tend to be few and far between and sometimes short-lived. This is unlikely to be the case for Ecoute! Ecoute! on both counts. Christian Biecher's design was rolled out to 15 sites just 18 months after the first store opened. The French store is all about hearing and audio.

As the supermarkets and hypermarkets around the world tighten their grip on an ever-increasing variety of product ranges, old-fashioned specialist retailers from cycle shops to stationers are feeling the pinch. In the light of this, perhaps a new generation of ever more particular and niche outlets will spring up on our shopping streets.

Skeen

PARIS, FRANCE
EMMANUEL FENASSE WITH F+B AGENCY

After ten years as a dermatological brand marketing director at L'Oreal, Pedro Garcia Maggi felt he knew a thing or two about the men's market, and he wasn't that impressed. 'I was very annoyed with the way in which men were treated like kids. The semantic always talks about the power of skin. It's a bit humiliating. Packaging is always blue or chrome, like a car. I think that's very outdated.' Skeen is his antidote to all this. At his store on the Marais, he's trying to reinvent the way male skincare is perceived: 'We don't treat men just as sportsmen.'

Maggi defines his offer as a dermo-cosmetic brand focusing on anti-ageing in male skin – the first of its kind. Before he opened the shop in 2006 on rue des Archives, Skeen products were just being sold through the cosmetics retailer Sephora and online. Now, his outlet is attracting people from the Marais – meaning the trendy, the well off and the gay. At weekends, the customer profile shifts somewhat as men come in with their wives and children.

The interiors are described by Emmanuel Fenasse as 'modern, simple, warm, welcoming and not too

"designed"'. This feeling is created by the use of natural materials like wood, the straw doormat and some black elements to respond to the Skeen products in a mainly white space.

Given Maggi's disillusionment with much of the men's skincare market, Skeen's packaging was seen as an opportunity to distance itself – literally – from the rest of the pack. Graphic designer Alejandra Rodriguez suggested some very simple matt black plastic containers which she branded with colour-coded stickers on the front, using old-fashioned, typewriter-style lettering. The aim was to create an air of efficacy around the products. 'We plan to use black as a powerful brand signature,' says Fenasse and, indeed, it is well exploited in the layout. Each of the 12 products, each recognizable by a colour, has its own column in the wall display. The product name is written vertically on what Fenasse calls the black bookmarks. 'It's a real wall of products; all the shelves are the same size, made of wood and are placed from floor to ceiling. We wanted to give the impression of profusion… like a grocery,' he adds.

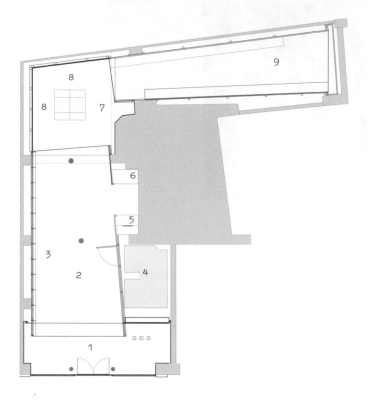

Left
Plan
1 Reception
2 Retail space
3 Product display
4 Stairs to cellar
5 Cash register
6 Closet
7 Diagnostic table
8 Black mirror
9 Projection space

Below
The typewriter- style
lettering on the
packaging is intended
to suggest efficacy.

Right
Fenasse replaced the
existing skylight with
16 hanging lamps.

Fenasse had three spaces to play with, and gave each a
different role: a selling space at the front, a diagnostic
space and a gallery room complete with video projection
in the middle, and a workshop and product animation
area. 'Behind the street's black façade we created a
huge white entrance with a high ceiling. There is strong
brand communication via a light box, which manages not
to disrupt the view into the shop,' explains Fenasse.
Little touches of theatricality include a big black
mirror which reflects the street scene on to the back wall
of the diagnostic area, and a black arch, which takes
customers through to the all- white gallery room. The
middle space originally had a skylight but Fenasse felt
that he couldn't keep the natural light. Instead he lit the
diagnostic table by 16 hanging lamps which 'allowed
a continuous ceiling height across all three spaces'.

Just a few months into opening, Maggi was struggling to
keep up with demand, even from women who have turned out to
be a surprise customer group. And he has already had ideas
about expansion: 'I would like to open more, maybe in other
European capitals. But first I want to see how this goes.'

theFLOWmarket

COPENHAGEN, DENMARK
MADS HAGSTRØM

What started out as a conceptual experiment has evolved into a retail offer, much to the surprise of its founder. theFlOWmarket is the brainchild of Mads Hagstrøm, a product designer by education. 'I wish to inspire people to think, consume and live more holistically,' he says. 'Consumerism can be a powerful way to affect the world.' He gives the example of his decision to buy organic food rather than conventional food: 'When I do that I support my own health (no pesticides or genetically modified crops), I support a healthy society (Fair Trade) and I support care for natural resources (animal welfare, careful growing methods, heat).'

He has translated his outlook into theFLOWmarket, a store-cum-installation in the Danish Design Centre. The environment's overall look is intended to exude a pure and cathedral-like ambience. Furnishing is minimal, with white drapes acting as walls and products sitting on industrial-style stainless-steel shelving. The products themselves give a knowing nod towards our rabidly consumerist society. Hagstrøm describes theFLOWmarket as a supermarket selling consumer awareness. This ethos is manifested in products whose aesthetically designed

packaging carries what he describes as humorous and thought-awakening labels. These items are sold for $5 to $20. The bottles and containers couldn't be simpler, their messages reading 'silence', 'tolerance', 'unconditional love' and such in black Helvetica type. The consumer surprise comes in the fact that every container is empty. It's a retail joke that theFLOWmarket's clientele seem happy to buy into.

'theFLOWmarket is basically me sharing my own problems and views with the world in a very basic way. That's why I think it is leaning very much towards an art installation. That's what is wonderful about design: it contains art, business and social entrepreneurship,' its creator adds.

Despite his initially uncommercial intentions, his plan now is to franchise the concept to other countries. 'So far I've had two design bureaux from Taipei, Taiwan and from Caracas, Venezuela who wish to create the same. I also lease or create versions for fairs and conferences.'

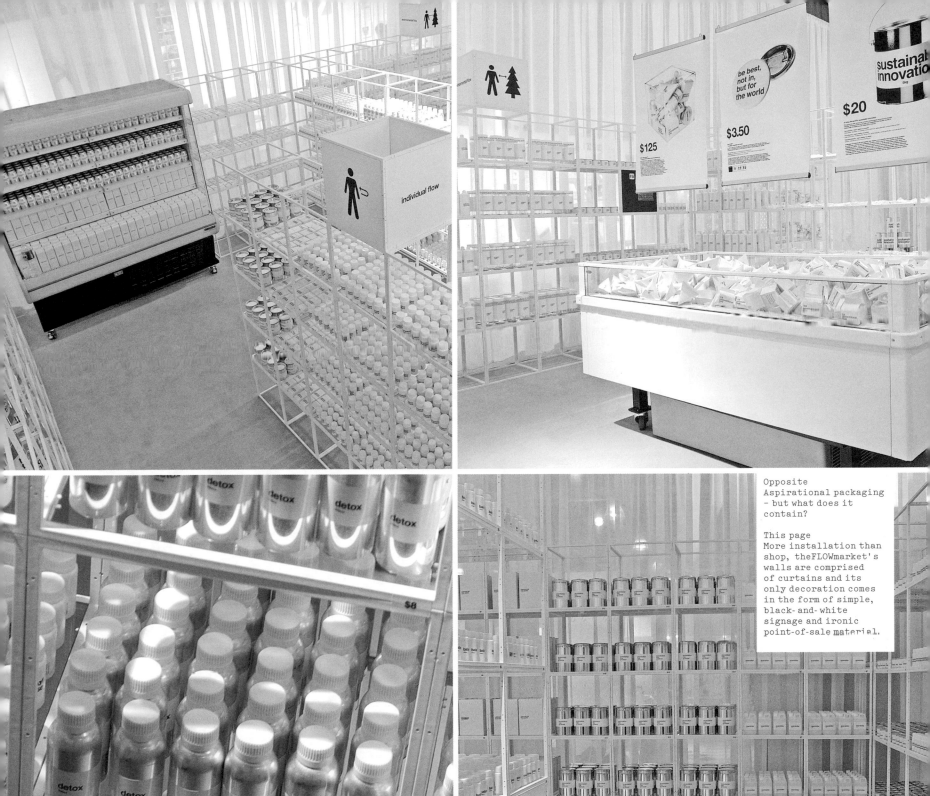

individual flow

be best,
not in,
but for
the world

$125 $3.50 $20

sustainab
innovatio

detox

$8

Opposite
Aspirational packaging
– but what does it
contain?

This page
More installation than
shop, theFLOWmarket's
walls are comprised
of curtains and its
only decoration comes
in the form of simple,
black- and- white
signage and ironic
point-of-sale material.

BooksActually

SINGAPORE, KAREN WAI AND KENNY LECK

'The design concept is purely based on our interpretation of childhood memories,' says Kenny Leck of the book shop he set up with Karen Wai on the first floor of an old shop-house. The duo coupled that nostalgia with their preference for European tastes and lifestyles, 'or so we think, according to the books we read!'. This means the idea of whiling away whole afternoons sitting cross-legged by tall glass windows reading novels, while taking tea and shortbread.

To re-create this, Leck and Wai installed long glass windows, with sticker decals depicting a pair of children reading atop trees, a castle and various fairy-tale animals. The white and green colour scheme is intended to evoke milk and apples. And the wooden flooring 'is wonderful for walking around barefoot, and the creaking of the floorboards is extremely delightful,' Leck adds. 'All these little experiences are very similar to warm summer afternoons of our childhood.'

In terms of merchandising, the approach was simple and efficient. The bookshelves are wall-mounted to free up the limited floor space, allowing the book spines to double as wallpaper. The rest of the decoration is drawn from the founders' own ephemera: glass jars of flavoured tea, vintage typewriters, bird cages suspended on ribbons from the ceiling, cream-coloured toy animals, tin boxes, cameras, antique Penguin paperbacks, film canisters, baby pianos and accordions. It all contributes to making this a very personal space, and a contrast to its nearby chain-store competition from Kinokuniya and Borders.

BooksActually opened in 2005 on the back of a mutual dream to set up a small independent book shop, 'no matter how incredible it seemed at that moment', says Leck. While Wai was studying English literature in Singapore at the time of writing this book, Leck had spent a couple of stints working at Tower Books and Borders.

The store, on Telok Ayer Street in Chinatown, is within five minutes' walking distance of the Singapore Central Business District. 'The area has a good mix of design creative agencies, architects, advertising houses and media agencies,' says Leck, so it must make up much of BooksActually's target market.

Because this is a concept book shop specializing in fiction and literature, the emphasis is on the classics and obscure and forgotten works. There is also Singapore-published prose and poetry on the shelves. Other delights include tasteful notebooks – including the hand-stitched in-house range – and stylish magazines.

Top left
This shop is all about books, with tightly packed floor-to-ceiling shelving. In front, side tables are stacked to form display units for books and other ephemera.

Left
Brightly coloured Olivetti typewriters are displayed underneath the bookshelves.

Centre left
The shop's literary stock extends to hand-crafted bookmarks.

Far left
Another intriguing BooksActually treat: single poems typed and compiled on sheets of grid paper and hand-bound.

Breathe

BERLIN, GERMANY, ROOMSAFARI

The Breathe concept is born out of the owner's desire
to break the mould and focus on niche brands. So it's
a premium offer, with the appropriate design cues.

Roomsafari, also based in Berlin, was responsible
for the name, interior design and identity. The name
signifies lightness, oxygen and freshness, explains
Christine Nogtev at Roomsafari. 'It also stands for
the desire to leave stressful everyday life behind, to
take a deep refreshing breath.' So the consultancy's
buzzwords were simplicity, transparency and elegance,
translated into fresh, warm and natural colours and
materials, and what Nogtev calls surprising and playful
presentations. 'We tried to transfer Breathe's high
class positioning to all parts of the interior, and
communication,' which means a soft, curved logotype
in the colours of fresh grass.

Opposite
The distinctive curved
logotype is intended
to convey lightness,
transparency and
elegance.

Above
Roomsafari has played
with the use of light on
the white background
to bring the products
to life.

The designers set about creating an ambience around
the idea of 'a short holiday in the countryside'. Hence
the display units featuring opaque glass (representing
water), pebbles (for the beach), natural grass (for
a meadow) and American nut wood (for a forest). These
natural cues are particularly appropriate since
Breathe's owner, Gregor Vidzer, quickly dispensed with
'high-tech' cosmetic stock in favour of focusing on
organic products. But natural does have its drawbacks
in interior design terms. 'We started with fresh grass
on the counter but after two weeks it looked like brown
seaweed,' he admits. The grass was replaced
with pebbles.

Roomsafari has played with light in this white space.
The merchandising walls are back-lit and appear to
glow, while overhead lamps illuminate the products
more precisely. 'The even light and accentuated light
are intended to support the atmosphere,' explains
Nogtev.

Vidzer worked for Lancaster Group for more than ten
years, and founded Breathe in 2002 as he wanted to set
up his own business rather than move to another big
business: 'I didn't want to focus on major commercial
brands, but rather on special niche brands that were
not stocked widely in Germany.'

Breathe is located on Berlin's Hackescher Markt
and is surrounded by one-off stores and high-end
international boutiques. Vidzer has no intention of
extending Breathe: 'The market is very small for what
we do.'

Ecoute! Ecoute!

PARIS, FRANCE
CHRISTIAN BIECHER & ASSOCIÉS

The concept of this store breaks the mould in two respects. It's a genuinely innovative offer – selling items to improve hearing and audio – and it's gone from a one-off to a chain in the blink of an eye. No sooner had the first Christian Biecher-designed store opened in Paris than Ecoute! Ecoute!'s founders were planning if not world-, then country-wide domination. In just 18 months they had a dozen stores, with their sights set on a 150-strong chain. Perhaps these are the lengths they must go to if they want to take on France's two market leaders, as these account for 25 per cent of the market.

French law forbids the sale of actual hearing aids in such stores, so Ecoute! Ecoute! sticks to what it calls 'comfort items', such as iPods and customized cell phones. Its president, Phillipe Mondan, who was CEO of French books and music chain Fnac, started the business with an audiologist and a hearing technology manufacturer. 'We three founders thought that hearing improvement was slow to develop for many reasons, including the fact that retailing shows poor customer performance. Our concept is dedicated to mobile hearing technology. With lower prices and better fitting processes, our non-medical store plays a role in removing inhibitions and promoting the joy of hearing,' he explains.

la douche sonore

le simulateur ambiophonique

les écouteurs multimédia

tout le monde en parle

iPod

'Ecoute! Ecoute! stores express a modern vision of an interior architecture of simple volumes floating in space, expressed with a specific use of colour and light,' says Biecher. He has designed the space in deference to the two components of music. 'The rhythm is expressed through the organization of volumes, the harmony is expressed through colour,' he adds. The site is structured around evenly spaced aluminium fixtures. Meanwhile, the yellow, green, blue, black and white boxes house computer games, hearing test stations, a soundproof studio and offices.

'Ecoute! Ecoute! is a totally innovative concept in terms of retail', states Biecher, 'so I was after a design that naturally expresses innovation with elegance and without any demonstrative element.'

Right
Offices are upstairs and retail is on the ground floor.

Below
Ground-floor plan
1 Entrance area
2 Product display
3 Stairs to basement
4 Listening area
5 Games consoles

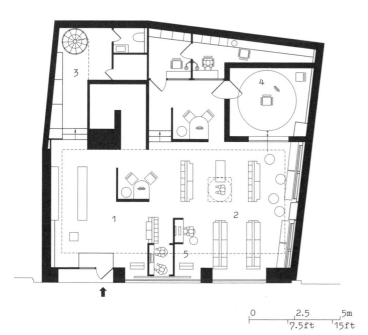

accueil auditien

les piles et les accus

l'assistance domestique

Evenly positioned
fixtures help define
the structure.

Left
The ground-floor retail
space is fitted out with
rough-hewn oak cabinets
and recessed, illuminated
shelving.

Below
The shop's sleek
own-brand packaging
features its distinctive
JHP-designed logo.

WholeMan

LONDON, UK
JHP DESIGN CONSULTANTS AND RAYLIAN

An unnamed high-net city banker was behind this concept.
As a frequent traveller, he saw a gap in the market 'for
a men's retail operation with conventional grooming, and
products that men increasingly have a use for,' explains
WholeMan's general manager, Peter Brockbank.

WholeMan is an entire concept, from products (including
an own-brand range of supplements and skincare and
grooming items) to treatments. On the ground floor, the
products are sold by trained naturopaths (those with
degrees in nutrition, health and alternative medicine)
and on the first floor, the treatment rooms offer
pedicures, massage, wet shaves and other services.
While JHP Design Consultants is responsible for the

retail concept, brand identity and packaging, Raylian
handled the detailed design and execution. The intention
is for WholeMan to lean towards performance rather than
beautification. Raylian's creative director, Nick Short,
describes the shopfront as masculine, with its black,
dark brown and yellow colour palette. Raylian created
the airport-style graphic icons on the right side of the
fascia, which are intended to draw would-be customers.
The door handle, which harks back to traditional men's
grooming, is in red and white striped twisted glass,
like an old-fashioned barber's pole.

The ground floor ceiling was painted dark brown, to make
it feel lower, according to Short. The counter was
created from roughed-up solid oak, to give the impression
of driftwood, and the glass countertop covers flat
white pebbles, emphasizing the natural beach feel. The
shelving is designed to be mobile, to allow for changes
in product ranges and quantities. Steve Collis, at JHP,
says: 'The packaging is sleek and black with subtle
references to the periodic table and the reassurance of
science.'

The first floor is reached via a spiral staircase - not a new addition but something that Raylian actually installed in this site a dozen or so years ago for the previous tenant Escada. Above it are surface-mounted, double-cluster low-voltage ceiling lights. The upstairs reception area is dashed out with bright orange Hitch Mylius chairs. Private, tranquil treatment rooms, where the JHP-designed logo is repeated on black glass walls, are placed at the front and back of this space.

Brockbank is not expecting to make money out of the first site in Mayfair. The plan is to open two more WholeMan shops in London; the first in Canary Wharf, to be quickly followed by another on the King's Road. Manchester, Birmingham, Glasgow, Edinburgh and Newcastle are next in line, with long-term plans for opening WholeMan shops in airport terminals. 'In three years we want to have 20 to 25 sites,' Brockman explains.

Franco oculista

BRAGA, PORTUGAL
JOSÉ MANUEL CARVALHO ARAÚJO

These interiors, which opened in the northern Portugese city of Braga in 2006, have more in common with a gentleman's club than a conventional eyewear shop. Nor do they have much in common with their former use. Before owner Jorge Castro Franco took on this space, it housed a shop selling Chinese and oriental paraphernalia.

Architect José Manuel Carvalho Araújo claims that the design reflects Franco, or at least Araújo's reading of him. 'The work was thought of from the very beginning in an innovative way, from the storage to the final assistance to the client, reflecting an idea of a new kind of store, closer to the notion of the "lounge", a space where we desire to remain, 'explains Carvalho Araújo.

Left
Unobtrusive vertical
branding alerts Braga's
style-conscious to this
venture.

Below left
The bold orange counter
contrasts with the
interior's tasteful
gloom.

Right
These pieces suggest
a gentleman's club or
lounge rather than an
eyewear shop.

Below
The store's logo offers
a subtle hint at what is
found inside.

The intention is to focus on the well-heeled customer rather than the designer frames themselves, hence the discreet wall-to-ceiling fitted drawers, which keep the stock hidden for much of the time. But there are flashes of an extrovert nature within the tasteful gloom, such as the antique-style chairs upholstered in vibrant florals, and an ornate gilt mirror. Despite the opulent styling, Franco oculista was fitted-out on a strict budget. Designer Pedro America, who worked with Carvalho Araújo on the scheme, points out that the low cost materials include a fishing net ('which is used to cover some construction mistakes'), and the crafty use of unfinished black MDF. The floor is painted concrete and bitumen – a type of hard coal.

It seems that most of the designers' time and creative effort went into the storage, and it has paid off. The specially designed sliding wall is made of MDF boxes and a metallic structure mounted on pull-out metallic frames, similar to the pharmacy storage closets, America explains. 'The closet is divided in two parts. In the upper part we have drawers to store the boxes, and in the lower part, boards with foam are mounted to store the actual glasses.' These boards can be taken out of their drawers and shown to the customer.

An unusual combination of both old and new optical machines is on show, and eye tests are performed on the first floor.

For the owner, who is an optometrist and optician, this is his second outlet in Braga. The first is much smaller, and in a completely different style. Franco says he has no intention of opening further stores.

Left
All eye tests are
carried out upstairs,
away from the club-like
waiting area.

Right
The stock is hidden away
in specially designed
sliding cabinets.

Pause Ljud & Bild

Pause Ljud & Bild (Swedish for 'sound and picture') is a reinvention of owner Fredrik Hjelmqvist's original retail enterprise. Previously called Sound Store, the shop was given its current name in 2000, and in 2004 this change was complemented by a complete interior overhaul, courtesy of Stockholm-based BAS Brand Identity.

Hjelmqvist's goal is to make Pause the country's leading retail brand in home entertainment, and it is he who hand-picks the electronic products on the shelves. He lists the Pause values as being knowledge, humour and the passion for picture and sound.

BAS set out to make the original warehouse-style stores more welcoming and user friendly. 'It also had to feel exclusive to attract the fastidious target audience, while not excluding the average customer,' says Björn Drawfarc at BAS.

The designers' solution was what they call a 'temple' to entertainment, which they created along the lines of 'exclusive punk'. Hence their mixing of unlikely elements, such as cardboard boxes, velvet and rococo chairs. While it was important for BAS not to stray too far from the previous look – they didn't want to scare away the loyal male customers – at the same time, many customers – especially some women – were known to be intimidated when shopping for such electronics. 'One of the challenges in this project was to simplify and demystify buying home electronic products,' Drawfarc adds.

BAS's solution was to install a 'glossary wall' answering such questions as 'What is a hi-fi nerd?' and 'Why should I buy a plasma?' As well as being informative, the wall is intended to inject a bit of humour into the environment.

Meanwhile, there's personal input in the shape of the point-of-sale material. Handwritten comments from staff might read: 'Fredrik says: probably the best plasma on the market right now.'

As is typical in such specialist stores, the staff are all-important in delivering the message. Here, the assistants are chosen for their almost nerdy obsessions with great sound and picture, or, as Hjelmqvist puts it: 'Our staff are experts "living hi-fi" 24/7.'

The bespoke listening post of acrylic and steel is back-lit.

The shop is divided into different room sets, 'creating a journey of discovery where customers experience something new around every corner,' says Drawfarc. So the cinema room makes references to a real cinematic experience, with floor lighting, rich, plush carpet, a velvet curtain and even the smell of popcorn. There's a guide to Pause's top 100 films, along with framed photos of Pause heroes – famous customers calling themselves 'audiofiler' (that is, people who are ridiculously fixated with excellent hi-fi).

The most exclusive equipment is on show in two smart but inviting VIP rooms, one black and one white, following the theory that the more money you plan to spend, the posher it gets. The white room goes by the name of the 'gold basement', and here the equipment is the most expensive you can find on the Swedish market. Features in this room include a padded wall, with tongue-in-cheek group shots of Hjelmqvist and his staff.

Hjelmqvist is planning to expand beyond his three Stockholm stores to perhaps Gothenburg or Malmö. 'I would like between seven and ten stores in five years' time,' he says, stressing that, 'I will grow slowly as I'm financing everything myself.'

Below left
The 'glossary wall' was installed to help demystify home entertainment equipment.

Below
The technique for the counter – a wooden framework covered in coated cardboard – is repeated for other furniture pieces around the store.

Right
The cinema room boasts floor lighting, a plush carpet and even the aroma of popcorn.

Bottom right
One of the two VIP rooms. The other is black.

CHAPTER 5
PRETENDERS AND GUERRILLA STORES

Conventional marketing techniques are all well and good when you are targeting a conventional consumer, but if you're after a group that occupies an edgy subculture, the perceived wisdom is that the unexpected is called for. Hence, the rise of the guerrilla or pop-up store, and the occasional appearance of an unbranded outlet that breaks from the look of its chain. Guerrilla or pop-up stores are more prevalent. Adopted mainly by fashion or fashionable brands, these sites follow a loose set of rules that seem counter-intuitive to traditional retailing. They are usually off the main shopping street; they are short-lived – anything from a day to a number of months; rather than disguising a building's former use, they often play it up; they are not 'designed' but rather seemingly thrown together by art students or game such, and, most importantly, they are not expected to generate much in the way of sales.

It's PR that these sites are after as Gwen Morrison, of US retail consultancy The Store, explains: 'These stores are mostly set up by higher-end brands trying to impact on the trend leaders, trying to link fashion with art. They are trying to create some sort of experience in a physical environment.' That is borne out by Spanish shoe brand Kowalski's activities in Asia-Pacific. 'It is mostly a branding exercise and a great way to stir interest in new markets,' says Olivia Dunn of Bold Initiatives, which is introducing the brand to the region through a string of pop-ups. Howard Saunders, at UK retail consultancy Echochamber, expects pop-ups to keep mushrooming. 'We will see it for brands that can cope with it,' he says, meaning trendy brands that can live with the space as it is. 'In the past, retailers have tended to dress up their stores, but we are sick of marketing hype and glossy environments. Nobody needs this stuff anyway.'

For a brand with a major reputation but a desire to be perceived differently, there's the risky but potentially rewarding unbranded outlet. These sites appear to deny all knowledge of their parent, and are likely to be mistaken for independent shops. They are the ultimate pretenders, paying a huge compliment to the independent retail sector. Orange's West London store 201 is a classic example. This is more of a chic boutique than a telecoms outlet. The colours are muted, the furniture is recycled and initially, at least,

there was hardly any marketing material on show – unheard of in the phone sector. Designed by section.d, this store is the antidote to phone shops. As Matthew Gayleard, who was at Orange at the time, says, 'There was a sense of intrigue for people, as they discovered it. People were coming in not even knowing that it was a phone shop.' Levi's departure into one-off stores resulted in some individually styled shops for its Red and Vintage Clothing collections. Jeff Kindleysides of Checkland Kindleysides, creators of the concept, admits that, 'There's a boredom factor in consumers' minds, and retail is in the doldrums. We have been pushing to get brands and retailers to think about different ways of engaging with consumers, such as nonbranded stores.' The consultancy's work for Levi's is widely regarded as opening the door for other retailers to follow.

However, for some in the industry, it makes little sense for a business to throw away all that hard-won brand awareness. 'I don't understand the logic of brand denial,' says Steve Collis of retail consultancy JHP. 'The unbranded approach is almost apologizing, it's pretending you are not who you are.' In his view, it makes more sense to set up a new brand if it's offering something new, or if it's got to appeal to a different audience.

In India, there's another take on the unbranded chain. Says architect Chris Lee, 'A lot of stores are designed and built without a designer, where the owner works directly with a contractor.' The result is more attention paid to the specifics of display, which are finely tuned to suit location. 'A lot of these stores have become chains but do not rely on a brand-driven aesthetic, changing with each location. This allows designers like us to concentrate on the performing intelligence of a store for a specific shopping environment.' Examples, says Lee's partner Kapil Gupta, are Sargam and Home Delite, which sells Indian snacks from kiosks, and traditional clothing stores such as Kala Nitetan, Roopam and Sheetal.

In developed markets pop-ups and unbranded shops work because they are relatively new, and so are generating the sort of media interest that makes them worthwhile. But if more brands jump on this bandwagon, their impact may become diluted as consumers start to suffer from guerrilla or pretender fatigue.

LEVI'S ICON STORES

LONDON, UK; MILAN, ITALY; BARCELONA, SPAIN;
PARIS, FRANCE AND BERLIN, GERMANY
CHECKLAND KINDLEYSIDES

At the beginning of the millennium, Levi's pioneered
a new form of retailing that has since been picked up
by a handful or more of fashion brands. The concept,
a sort of anti-chain chain, was originated by Checkland
Kindleysides, and was triggered by the fact that customer
segmentation was kicking in. Different sorts of customer
could no longer be guaranteed to patronize the same store.
'Customer segmentation was becoming more about physically
going out and delivering different expressions of your
brand to meet the right people head-on,' explains Jeff
Kindleysides of Checkland Kindleysides. And people, in
this context, means early adopters and opinion leaders.

So the consultancy was tasked with delivering this
experience from a retail point of view. Kindleysides
recalls that 'We drew a map of a fictitious town, showing
where the volume of customers was. We then drew a side
street off that, and a tiny street off that.' The thinking
behind such a secluded location was that customers would
have to actually find it and it would become a place they
would tell their friends about.

At the time, Newburgh Street, off London's Carnaby Street,
fitted the bill. 'Nothing was happening down there,'
Kindleysides says, so the rent was low. And this store
- Cinch - became Levi's first guerrilla store, carrying its
Red and Vintage Clothing collections.

Above
Cinch, London.
Product information
was 'home-made',
using polaroids and
labelling tape.

Left
Cinch, London. in the
Store's original
manifestation, the
chair and shelving
acted as the cash
desk. With no till,
the money was taken
in a cash tin.

Right
Cinch, London. Denim
design details were
sketched on the wall
in chalk.

In terms of Cinch's look, Kindleysides wanted it to appear as if it was owned by a couple of arty people who were passionate about denim – 'We got a graduate who was working for us to go down to the site with some guys from our workshop'. The graduate was briefed to imagine that it was his store and that he was going to run it with friends. The result, says Kindleysides, was like an art installation as 'there were no commercial considerations whatsoever'. It didn't even have a till, but a cash tin. The effect was naïve but appealing and, as a nonbranded store, it became a destination in its own right.

With the success of Cinch, Levi's started to be written about in the press in a different way, says Kindleysides. It also brought Checkland Kindleysides the most awards the consultancy had ever won for a single project.

Checkland Kindleysides followed Cinch up with individual, nonbranded Levi's stores across western Europe. 'We took the architecture that was there to make it into something that suited the locality,' Kindleysides adds. With each, it was about maintaining the feel of a small independent retailer. Hence B-Fly in Milan, (Z)ink in Barcelona, Nim in Paris and Buttenheim in Berlin. The sense of an exhibition space was achieved by leaving walls blank for emerging artists and photographers to display their work.

Since then, the Carnaby Street store has been redesigned by Checkland Kindleysides around an unravelling 'red thread' that is intended to symbolize the Red sub-brand.

Left
Cinch, London. This gallery space in the basement exhibited customized products and the work of young artists.

Above
The London store was redesigned around the theme of an unravelling red thread, which operates here as a hanging device.

Left
Buttenheim, Berlin.
The gallery space
is shown here with
projected films and
illuminated product
displays.

Below
Buttenheim, Berlin.
Of the shop's four
areas, this is the
front room, with a
relaxed, 'living
room' feel.

Bottom
Buttenheim, Berlin.
In one corner an old
camp bed is used as a
display unit.

Right
The black painted floor
of the gallery space
encroaches into the
plain plywood floor
of the retail space.

*esto me suena a chino!!

SWATCH INSTANT STORES

BARCELONA AND MADRID, SPAIN
LUCA MANES AND THILO BRUNNER
WITH PIXELPUNK

Left
The Swatch Instant sub-
brand has its own logo
– a graffitied corporate
marque overlaid with an
asterisk.

Bottom left
The exterior of the
Madrid Instant Store.

This page
The 'undesigned' nature
of Instant Stores is
intended to attract
people who slip under
the conventional retail

The powers that be at Swatch realized that the company
was missing a trick with its conventional retail
chain, in its failure to lure in those hard-to-pin-
down, subculture types so coveted by many a fashion
brand. 'Today's societies are moving and diversifying
with increasing speed, and the consumer is morphing
accordingly,' says Swatch's chief operating officer
Reto Stoeckli. 'Trends are coming and vanishing faster
and faster, often spreading simultaneously around the
globe. Conventional long-term stores do not normally
follow this fast-moving rhythm and diversity of which we
want to be a part.' So the brand has adopted a guerrilla
strategy, with a format that can be set up and dismantled
at top speed. 'They can pop up anywhere in the world where
a refreshing cultural scene is emerging, enjoy a brief,
intensive presence, then disappear and pop up again in a
different place,' Stoeckli adds.

Sites are chosen for their synchronicity with the brand and for their relevance to the target audience. And because of their nomadic interior approach and uncommercial raison d'être, they might appear for a year or more, or just for a day. 'They pop up in trendy boroughs in urban areas, at festivals or events, at the top of mountains or at the beach,' he says. So between the summers of 2005 and 2006, Instant Stores came and went in over 50 locations, including Berlin, Barcelona, London, Paris, Zurich, Amsterdam, Shanghai and Geneva. The idea is that they should be a surprise when they pop up. 'Who knows today where tomorrow the sub-culture will emerge and where unconventional trends will develop?' Stoeckli muses. Indeed, who would have thought that Amsterdam's Schipol Airport was such a destination, but the presence of an Instant there for four months in 2006 suggests this is the case.

In terms of interiors, these Instants comprise a handful of hexagonal merchandising units, and much 'decoration' courtesy of local graffiti artists or a similar group.

Left and right
The Instant Store in
Barcelona's Argenteria
had strong wall graphics,
created by Pixelpunk.

Bottom left
The merchandising unit
is based on a geometrical
form of two hexagons.

The two in Spain and a handful of others are the creation
of Pixelpunk (aka Olivier Rossel), who describes himself
as an independent illustrator and graphic designer
working out of Biel and Basel. The creative management of
each store design is masterminded by Luca Manes and Thilo
Brunner in Swatch's retail department. 'Their specially
designed furniture gives an additional edgy touch by
featuring only 60 and 120 degrees angles compared to
the 90 degrees angles found in traditional furniture
concepts,' explains Stoeckli. 'The shape of this
furniture gives us literally millions of possibilities
of how it can be put together.'

In terms of their commercial considerations, Stoeckli
admits that while till sales are still important, the
Instants' forte is as a marketing tool. 'The success
is measured by feedback from the media, but also from
opinion leaders, artists, designers, by a scene which is
credible and makes the product hype.' So far the concept
- as well as many of the stores themselves - has certainly
delivered as far as media coverage goes.

COMME DES GARÇONS GUERRILLA STORES

COLOGNE, GERMANY,
CHEWING THE SUN AND VARIOUS ARTISTS;
GLASGOW, UK, MUTLEY, STUDIO WAREHOUSE [SWG3]

Rei Kawakubo of Comme des Garçons is widely credited with introducing the brand's guerrilla store concept – a world away from the fashion house's sleek flaghip stores in New York, Paris, London and Japan. From the first guerrilla outpost in Berlin (2004-2005) to so-called interventions in Glasgow, Athens, Cologne and beyond, these shops are rough and ready in a studied way. Comme des Garçons' guidelines require that a guerrilla store should last no longer than a year in any location. Following these guidelines, each store's interior should also remain true to the host building's former use, in an effort to act as a magnet for young, style-conscious types. The guidelines also demand that the stock consist of vintage Comme des Garçons and new stock, chosen with the season and the spirit of the store's host city in mind.

The idea is that these spaces become destinations in their own right, promoted, as they are, by street posters and word of mouth rather than by conventional advertising. Locations are carefully sought out in parts of town that are edgy or buzzy, but which may have little other retail space around to entice shoppers. Eva Gödel of advertising design studio Chewing the Sun and creator of the Cologne store (September 2005 to October 2006), describes it as a highly dynamic, temporary space where 'people come in to meet other people and discover new ideas'.

The Cologne site had been, since the 1950s, a family-owned butcher's shop called Neffgen. Meanwhile, the shop in Glasgow was based in an old wedding-car garage on York Hill. 'We are far removed from the high street,' says visual artist Mutley, who ran the store during its existence from May 2006 to January 2007. 'It's still not a developed area.'

The people at Chewing the Sun, based in Wuppertal, Germany, were tasked with giving the Cologne outlet some pulling power. 'We invited artists to produce works in order to optimize the original look of the butcher's shop,' explains Gödel. To this end, Cologne-based artist Johannes Wohnseifer created an installation by changing the glass in the lighting and painting the door a particular shade of green made for Cologne's bridges over the Rhine. In the changing room Wohnseifer installed a showcase in which he rotated one of his favourite books, magazines or records on a weekly basis.

Gödel explains that – in accordance with the guerrilla store ethos – they used only the original butcher's shop fixtures and fittings. 'As the clothes were too many to put on the meat hangers we had two long racks made out of an original butcher's hanging bar. We made the changing room out of the curtain material that is used across the entrances of storage rooms to keep the cold in.'

Above
Artist Johannes Wohnseifer painted the door of the Cologne store the same colour as the city's bridges.

Opposite top, bottom and right
Changes are kept to a minimum, so this old butcher's shop is still in possession of its stained flooring, white tiles and copious meat hooks.

As Mutley points out, 'Comme des Garçons choose the spaces because of their historical purpose or current function, so they don't want you to change them much.' With this in mind, he 'decorated' the garage in Glasgow with a 1977 Daimler. After seeing the car and the space, local artist Jim Lambie proposed covering the Daimler in paisley vinyl. (The space is now Lambie's studio). Another artist, Benedict Radcliffe, decorated a Honda scooter for the store. As Mutley explains, 'We've turned the space into an installation, with horseshoes and anything we could find. We've created a garage feel but one that is clean and with fantastic product.' In terms of major construction work, Mutley only had to build a new interior wall. 'We're artists and didn't have any cash.'

At the time of going to press, three new guerrilla stores had just opened in Cracow, Hong Kong and Singapore.

Above, far left
Far from Glasgow's retail centre, this guerrilla store still manages to draw the crowds.

Above and left
In this former garage for wedding cars the centre of attention is the paisley-bedecked Daimler by Jim Lambie.

Left and below
A few posters and some
basic hanging rails
sit alongside ephemera
from the building's
previous use, creating
a raw environment with
some all-important
provenance.

KOWALSKI
POP-UP STORE

SYDNEY, AUSTRALIA
BOLD INITIATIVES PTY LTD

The Spanish are good at shoes. While high-profile Camper has many of its own stores, Kowalski tends to rely on department stores, boutiques and select online retail sites. They're also available through its own website, www.kowaslkishoes.com. A family-owned business for nearly 40 years, Kowalski's HQ is in the Spanish town of Elche.

Australia-based Bold Initiatives are the distributors for Kowalski in the Asia-Pacific region, and they needed to raise awareness of this unknown brand so that retailers and their customers would take an interest in it. Hence, Bold Initiatives is planning a succession of pop-up stores, the first of which appeared in the Paddington quarter of Sydney from April to June 2006. The idea of a pop-up is that it comes, gets a lot of attention, then goes. 'All the Asia-Pacific countries are new markets for the Kowalski brand, therefore a pop-up is a great way of introducing the brand and creating interest in the product, before "popping away" and leaving a gap in the market for other retailers to take on the brand (as they can see a demand has been created),' Olivia Dunn of Bold Initiatives explains.

Left and below left
Bold Initiatives
created a handmade
feel by literally
writing on the shop
window.

Right
The interiors are
studiedly shabby
chic, right down to
the shelving: planks
of wood appropriated
from a shipwreck.

Choice of site is vital for this exercise, as it's all about the right sort of high footfall. 'We are choosing sites with significant foot traffic. As Kowalski has never been seen before, you need people to be constantly passing by the store rather than creating a destination. The site still needs to be in an area which portrays the right image for the brand, so we selected a fashionable area renowned for higher-end, trendy designer brands,' explains Dunn.

Kowalski, which has turned the idea of shabby chic into an art form, demands suitably un-buffed interiors. Bold Initiatives, which created the Paddington outlet themselves, tried to reflect the brand's retro, American feel in the environment. 'As soon as people walked into our store, we needed them to associate Kowalski with vintage-inspired, retro, mismatched themes,' says Dunn. She opted to keep it very simple, and sourced furniture and furnishings from places such as flea markets, auctions and eBay, as well as second-hand and antique stores. She needed the outlet to look strong and portray the brand appropriately while being cost-effective, given its temporary nature.

Above and right
With table football set up in one corner and its so-tacky-they're-cool velour armchairs and matching footstool, this pop-up has the feeling of a student common room.

Left
The simple system of wall brackets can be used to support shelves or to hang merchandise, allowing for maximum flexibility.

Hence, the Paddington site's retro Spanish-cum-American look. Dunn lists the fixtures and fittings: mustard velour armchairs and footstools, a bright orange fluffy rug, table football, retro lamps and light shades, a beaten-up old wooden desk and chair, a 1960s wooden side table for the window display, and very simple shelving that was created from wood taken from a ship wreckage. 'These shelves were perfect as they were rustic and had blue paint flaking off, which is very suitable for the "distressed" Kowalski look,' she adds.

It was then down to PR, Kowalski's website, electronic mail-outs and good old word of mouth to spread the word among the fashionably aware.

From a brand awareness perspective, Paddington was very successful. Bold Initiatives measured their effect by the number of hits the brand's website then got from Australia. 'The number of visits from Australia increased significantly. It had been approximately the tenth ranked country (in terms of number of visitors), but for the duration of the pop-up and the month following, it was the number one ranked country (in terms of visitors).'

However, Dunn admits that Australia is not the most suitable market for pop-up retailing. 'If we were to do it again we would choose an area with significantly greater foot traffic. This is why we believe Asia would be a great option for pop-up,' she says, adding that she was planning some other locations for 2007.

201 WESTBOURNE GROVE (ORANGE SHOP)

LONDON, UK, SECTION.D

'We had an unwritten rule that you shouldn't be able to replace any furniture the next day.' This seems an extraordinary statement from the designers of a chain store, where homogenization and uniformity are de rigeur, but that is actually what has happened at one outlet of the telecoms shop Orange.

Alan Graham, at the Harrogate design agency section. d, was tasked with creating something that is usually anathema to telecoms chains: a one-off shop that didn't look like a phone shop, let alone an Orange phone shop. The reasoning for this departure came from Nick Moore and Matt Gayleard in Orange's retail division. 'Rolling out the same thing everywhere is not always the answer,' says Gayleard. 'You can't have one size fits all. Tailoring the retail environment to that customer in a specific catchment area is really important.'

Above
In its early days, 201's shopfront had no Orange logo. The delivery bike propped up in front also belies the store's true identity.

180

Above
One wall is covered
with pictures of
satisfied 201 customers
in a hotch-potch of
frames, some of which
were sourced from a
neighbouring framing
shop.

The area he was talking about is Westbourne Grove,
a funky, high-end street in Notting Hill that is
littered with one-off retailers and, more importantly
for Orange, other chains that are disinheriting
themselves from their parent groups. French Connection
and Nicole Farhi both have boutiques in the vicinity
without their names on the fascia. It is only when you
go in and start looking at the labels that you realize
everything is from the same brand. Gayleard elaborates
on the rationale: 'To put in the sort of phone shop
you would expect would have been the wrong thing to do
on Westbourne Grove, so we did the complete opposite
to a phone shop. Phones had become a lifestyle object
but the [usual phone] shops didn't reflect that. So the
brief to the designers was: not another phone shop.'
Moore and Gayleard asked section.d to consider how
they would sell these things if they were jewellery.
'We were after a boutique-chic, eclectic, home-made
feel,' Gayleard says.

section.d conjured up that feel by really going to
town - in an unchain-store way - with 201's fixtures and
fittings. 'Where we could, everything was recycled,
because our research showed that's what was called
for,' says Graham. After all, this is hippy, grungy
Notting Hill, where oh-so trendy boho types have
plenty of cash which they're not afraid to spend.
Hence, section.d's hard work in sourcing unusual
pieces. For example, lighting comes courtesy of a
dozen or so Herbert Terry Anglepoise lamps, some of
which were bought for £1 and some for £200. On a coffee
table at the front of the shop, flexible map-reading
light arms have been reconfigured to have phones
attached to them. The pièce de résistance is a large,
distressed unit. 'It's made of recycled furniture
which we collected in auctions and car boot sales,'
says Graham. 'We hacked it up and got a furniture
designer friend to put it back together again.' Within
this unit are a number of hidden drawers, each of
which reveals a live phone, laid neatly on a piece
of thick grey felt. These drawers had former lives
variously as an old army food box, a Victorian firebox,
and a container for a pig slapper (which was used for
branding pigs). 'Authenticity is the last bastion
of retail. This store is a nod in the direction of
something that's a little bit more real,' says Phil
Hobbis at section.d, 'not because it's been there for
years, but because you won't find it in Birmingham or
Leicester.'

Below
Variously sourced
Anglepoise lamps shed
light on the specially
built display unit.

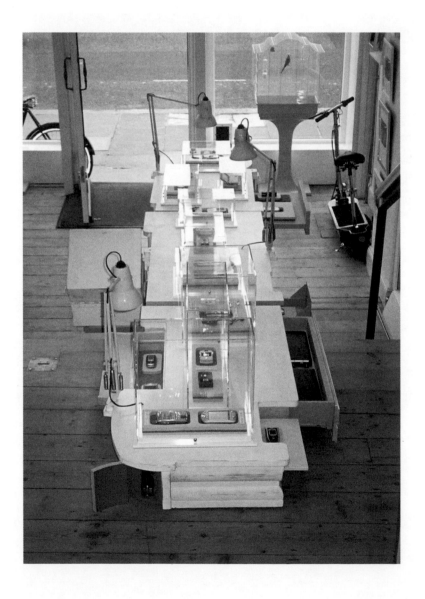

Like all dedicated designers, section.d would have liked to push the uniqueness of the shop even further. Vintage aircraft seats were sourced for the front of the store but Orange opted for swivel chairs (in orange), which look as though they could be replaced from a designer furniture shop within 24 hours.

For Orange, what really differentiates this store is its service culture. Although it has a low footfall, by putting their best staff in 201, which opened in 2005, the store has consistently achieved the highest transaction value and conversion rate of any of its outlets, says Gayleard. And amazingly, 201 was done 'under the radar' by Moore and Gayleard because, like all big business, most things are decided by committee and this would never have got through.

While section.d's reinvention of the chain will not be rolled out (and may not even last much longer after both Moore and Gayleard have left Orange), it has taught Orange and other chains some important lessons. As well as tailoring outlets to the locale, it has shown how much PR - none of which was courted - an innovation can generate. But whether shoppers will come to find this unbranded approach underhand and deceitful is another issue. Perhaps by pretending to be a one-off, chains could be seen to be intentionally misleading their potentially loyal customers.

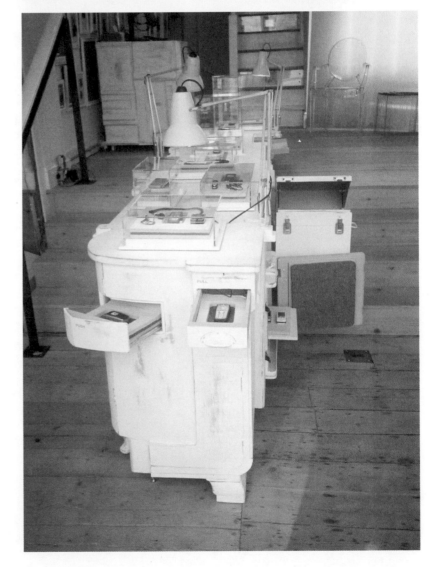

Top left and right
The unit incorporates recycled boxes and drawers, some of which formerly held army provisions and pig-branding devices.

Right
Each drawer reveals a live phone sitting on a neat bed of grey felt.

Index

Page numbers underlined refer
to picture captions

Project credits

2006 FEB01
Architect and interior designer:
BEHF
www.behf.at
Client:
Staudacher & Partner

201 WESTBOURNE GROVE (ORANGE SHOP)
Design:
Sam Cutting, Alan Graham, Phil Hobbis,
David McRae at section.d
www.section-d.com
Furniture construction:
Jonathan Ingleby, Sarah Drew
Sourcing, project management,
installation:
section.d
Client:
Matt Gayleard, Orange

ACRYLIC
Interior and exterior design:
KleinDytham architecture
www.klein-dytham.com
Client:
jewellery designer Masako Ban

ARTGADGETS
Design:
Maurer United Architects
www.maurerunited.com
Project team:
Marc Maurer, Nicole Maurer,
Gaby Vanhommerig, Rob Breuls,
Ellen van de Weerdt
Client:
Art Company, Eindhoven
Contractor, interior
Houta Bouw, Geldrop

Contractor, steel doors and plastic
furniture table:
Hupkens Industrial Models

BAKALIKO ALL THE BEST
Design:
Red Design Consultants
www.reddesignconsultants.com
Client Service Director:
Gina Senduka
Creative Director:
Rodanthi Senduka
Designers:
Rodanthi Senduka, George Perdikoulis,
Sofia Georgopoulou, Eleni Masselou
Copywriter:
Giannis Andonopoulos
Production Supervisor:
George Perdikoulis

BOOKSACTUALLY
Interior design:
Karen Wai and Kenny Leck
www.booksactually.com
Client:
BooksActually

BOULE
Interior Designer:
Michelle Myers
Architect:
Ralph Gentile Architects
Display cases:
Ciam, part of the Arredo Group S.P.A.
Client:
Food Art Group, LLC

BREATHE
Design:
Roomsafari
Client:
www.breathe-cosmetics.com

CHAN LUU
Architect:
Marmol Radziner + Associates
www.marmol-radziner.com
Principals:
Leo Marmol, FAIA and Ron Radziner, FAIA
Project Manager:
Stephanie Hobbs
Project Architect:
Aaron Brode

COMME DES GARÇONS, COLOGNE
Comme des Garçons

COMME DES GARÇONS, GLASGOW (GUERRILLA STORE +44 141)
Curator:
Mutley, Studio Warehouse [SWG3]
www.swg3.tv

THE CORNER BERLIN
Concept and Interior Design:
Emmanuel de Bayser and Josef Voelk
www.thecornerberlin.de
Architect:
Gonzalez Haase

DELICATESSEN
Design:
Z-A/Guy Zucker
www.guyzucker.com
Clients:
Delicatessen/Idit Barak
and Sharon Gurel

DESIGN REPUBLIC
Architectural and interior designer:
Neri & Hu Design and Research Office
(NHDRO)
www.neriandhu.com
Partners-in-charge:
Lyndon Neri and Rossana Hu

Project team:
Gary Chan, Erica Lanselle, Windy Zhang,
Joy Qiao

ECOUTE! ECOUTE!
Interior architect:
Christian Biecher & Associés –
Christian Biecher assisted by
Céline Trétout
www.biecher.com
Client:
Ecoute! Ecoute!

FENTONS GOURMET
Architect:
Derrick KL Tsang
Graphic designer:
Lau Kwok Fai

FISHES
Design:
Studio Linse Amsterdam
www.studiolinse.com
Client:
Fishes - Bart van Olphen
Contractor:
Xander Bueno de Mesquita

THEFLOWMARKET
Design:
Mads Hagstrøm
www.theflowinstitute.com
www.theflowmarket.com

FRANCO OCULISTA
Design:
José Manuel Carvalho Araújo, arch.
www.carvalhoaraujo.com
Project team:
Pedro America, designer; Alexandre
Branco, architect; Xavier Coennen,
designer

FRIEND
Design:
Yves Béhar/fuseproject, Johan Liden
www.fuseproject.com

GARAGE
Architect:
Zaiga Gaile - SIA Zaigas Gailes Birojs
Designers:
Laima Kaugure, Franceska Kirke

GOŬ
Interior designer/architect:
Marina Younan
Client:
Noyau s.a.r.l.

GRASSHOPPER
Architect:
Dyan Belliappa

GUYS & DOLLS
Architect:
Sybarite, London (Simon Mitchell,
Torquil McIntosh, Iain Mackay & Eliana
Voutsadakis)
www.sybarite-uk.com
Client:
Guys & Dolls, London (Sarah Ettedgui,
Sabrina Ettedgui)
Main contractor:
Purple Shopfitters, London (Kevin Dansie,
Derek Kennedy)
Specialist joinery:
Arredo Deco, Italy (Massimiliano Tiezzi)
Security:
Knighthood Securities, London
(Hugh Murray)
Glazing/metalwork:
Metal Deco, Italy (Andrea Tiripelli)
Acrylic domes:
Talbot Designs, London (Charles Woolf)

Landscaping:
Earthmoves, London (Deborah Haynes)

ISOLÉE
Designer:
Teresa Sapey Architecture Studio
www.teresasapey.com
Collaborators:
Interior design: Angela Sanz, Marta
Melendo, Raquel Rojas, Antjo Stuohlik
Enviromental graphics: Alex Gutwil

KOWALSKI POP-UP STORE
Design, sourcing of materials and fit-out:
Bold Initiatives Pty Ltd
www.boldinitiatives.com.au
Creative marketing:
Omelette Creative

LEVI'S ICON STORES
Design:
Checkland Kindleysides
www.checkind.com

MELT
Architect:
Michaelis Boyd Associates
www.michaelisboyd.com
Owner-founder:
Louise Nason
Master Chocolatier:
Keith Hurdman

MERCADO MODERNO
Design:
Marcelo Vasconcellos and Alberto Vicente
www.mercadomodernobrasil.com.br

NICHOLAS JAMES
Design:
Giddings Design
www.giddingsdesign.com

Shopfit:
Benbow Interiors

ONE
One concept:
Bleed
www.bleed.no
One logo:
Kjetil Wold

PAPABUBBLE
Barcelona:
Interior design: Christopher King
and Tommy Tang
Graphic design/packaging: Christopher King
Client: Papabubble sl (Christopher King
and Tommy Tang)
Amsterdam:
Interior design and architect: Domonic Otto
Graphic design: Christopher King
Client: Papabubble nl
Tokyo:
Interior design: Christopher King
Graphic design: Christopher King
Client: Papabubble jp
www.papabubble.com

PAUSE LJUD & BILD
Design:
BAS Brand Identity
www.basbrandidentity.se

PLATFORM SOUL
Design:
Keane + Timm – Patrick Keane,
Christoph Timm, Feng Jiang,
Leslie Barbiero

PRINCI
Design architect:
Claudio Silvestrin architects
www.claudiosilvestrin.com

Design team:
Principal: Claudio Silvestrin
Architects team: Mariachiara Suriani,
Fabrizio Cellini, Laura Lupini
Site architect: Studio Ferrari Ardicini
Structural engineers: Ricerca&Progetto
Lighting: Claudio Silvestrin architects
with Viabizzuno
Air-conditioning engineers: LMConsulenze
Building firm: Impresa Fratelli Panigoni
Shop fitters: Studiotre Contract
Brick oven: S. A. R. L. Fours Voisin

PURPLE SHOP
Interior design and graphics
on the walls:
M41LH2/Johanna Hyrkäs
www.m41lh2.com

SKEEN
Architectural design:
Emmanuel Fenasse with F +B Agency
Art and graphic designer:
Alejandra Rodriguez

SLICE
Architectural and interior designer:
Neri & Hu Design and Research Office
(NHDRO)
www.neriandhu.com
Partners-in-charge:
Lyndon Neri and Rossana Hu
Associate-in-charge:
Andrew Roman
Project team:
Abigail Cua, Windy Zhang

STYLE: NORDIC
Design:
Jonas Ericsson
www.stylenordic.com

SWATCH INSTANT STORES
Design, decorations, illustrations,
installations and execution:
Luca Manes and Thilo Brunner

THANKS
Architects:
Chris Lee and Kapil Gupta
Project team:
London: Mariana Ibanez, Armando Elias,
Yael Gilad
Mumbai: Advait Potnis, Shailesh
Karangutkar, Namita Dharia, Adarsh
Akella, Hemant Purohit, Renu Gupta,
Santosh Thorat, Aaron Minz
Project management: Chesterton Meghraj
Service consultants: Rohit Uchill
(services), Shashank Mahendale
(structural design), Anil Walia
(lighting design)
Contractors: Kaisher Interiors,
Mody Interiors, Bhushan Sales
(air-conditioning), Light Options
& Gemini Global (lighting)

WHOLEMAN
Corporate identity:
JHP Design Consultants
www.jhp-design.com
Shop fitting:
Raylian Design

Picture Credits

(7) Andrew Moran
(8 left) © Alan Schein Photography/Corbis
(8 right) © Noah Addis/Star Ledger/Corbis
(9) Powerline 6
(10) Matteo Piazza
(11) Lluís Capdevila Martín
(12) Fredrika Lökholm
(13) Andrew Moran
(16-19) Stefanos Samios/Studio Phobia
(20-22) Mark Takahashi
(23) Michelle Myers
(24-27) Teo Krijgsman
(28-29) Tommy Tang (Barcelona), Domonic
Otto (Amsterdam), Christopher King (Tokyo)
(30-32) Richard Lewisohn
(33 left) Richard Lewisohn
(33 right) James Bedford
(34-35) Graham Uden
(36-37) Michel Esta
(38-40) Derryck Menere
(41 top left and right) Derryck Menere
(41 bottom) NHDRO
(42-45) Matteo Piazza
(48-51) Sylvain Cherkaoui
(51 bottom right) Pablo Orcajo
(52-53) Pablo Orcajo
(54-57) Christopher A, Ditto Studios,
Singapore
(58-61) Chris Harisson
(62) Derryck Menere
(63 top) Derryck Menere
(63 bottom) NHDRO
(64-67) Derryck Menere
(68-71) André Nazareth
(72-75) Sergejs Kondrasins
(76-81) Sven Wiederholt
(82-85) Maarten van Viegen
(88-93) Fram Petit
(94) Daici Ano
(95) Masako Ban
(96-101) Glen Gooch at Moodswing Media
(102-105) Christoph Timm

(106-109) Naomi Yogev and Shay Ben-Efraim
(110-111) Benny Chan/fotoworks
(112-114) Adrian Myers
(115 left) Fredrika Lökholm
(115 right) Adrian Myers
(116-117) A. Muehe
(118) H. Maier
(119 top and bottom left) H. Maier
(119 bottom right) A. Muehe
(120-123) Bruno Klomfar
(124-127) Pallon Daruwala
(128-129) Matti Pyykkö
(132-135) Skeen
(136-137) Niclas Jessen
(138-139) BooksActually
(140-143) www.breathe-cosmetics.com
(144-147) Luc Boegly
(148) Elaine Duigenan
(149) Fredrika Lökholm
(150-151) Elaine Duigenan
(152-155) Hugo Carvalho Araújo
(156-159) Per Ranung
(162-165) Jon Arnold
(166-167) Robertino Nikolic
(168-171) Swatch
(172-173) Comme des Garçons
(174 left) Andy Kennedy
(174 right) Mark Dickie
(174 bottom) www.sweeneypix.com
(175 top left and right) Andy Kennedy
(175 bottom left and right)
www.weskingston.com
(176-179) pictures supplied
by www.echochamber.com
(180-182) Wim Hoogstraten
(183 left) Phil Hobbis
(183 right) Wim Hoogstraten

The author would like to thank the
following for their inspiration,
support, or both:

Tom Dixon
Emma Moore, <u>Wallpaper</u>* magazine
Howard Saunders, Echochamber
Lucy Johnston, GDR
Richard Perks, Mintel
Gwen Morrison, The Store
Steve Collis, JHP
Claudia Saraiva
Daven Wu